DENNIS TAY
Natural Break

DENNIS TAYLOR
Natural Break

Macdonald
Queen Anne Press

A Queen Anne Press BOOK

First published in hardcover in 1985 by Queen Anne Press,
a division of Macdonald & Co (Publishers) Ltd
Maxwell House, 74 Worship Street, London EC2A 2EN
A BPCC plc Company
Reprinted 1986
This edition first published in 1986

Illustrations by Graham Thompson
Photographs by David Muscroft
Designed by David Grogan

British Library Cataloguing in Publication Data

Taylor, Dennis, 1948–
Natural break
    1. Snooker – Anecdotes, facetiae, satire, etc.
    I. Title
    794.7'35'0207   GV900.S6

ISBN 0 356 12566 1

Typeset by J & L Composition Ltd, Filey, North Yorkshire
Printed in Great Britain by
Hazell Watson & Viney Limited,
Member of the BPCC Group,
Aylesbury, Bucks

Contents

Foreword by Steve Davis

THE 1984–85 snooker season was without doubt a most incredible year for Dennis Taylor. In a professional career spanning thirteen years he has been without question one of the most consistent and hardworking players, and of course to win the World Championship after trailing 0–8 to yours truly is an achievement which I believe ranks him as one of the all-time greats. We have had many great meetings since I turned professional in 1978 and honours are pretty well even so far; his 1985 success makes the score between us in World Championships 2– 2! I will obviously be trying to go ahead in the years to come, but I know from experience that it is not going to be easy.

There is, though, a completely different side to Dennis Taylor and *Natural Break* sums him up perfectly – a comedian in a dress-suit! Dennis has kept us all in stitches on the professional circuit during the past dozen or so years, and despite wins or losses his attitude has always been the same – let's make it fun!

This book not only relates well-known and lesser-known 'Dennis Taylor' stories, it also speaks volumes of the man himself – a great player and a very funny person.

Long may they both prosper.

Introduction

IT'S taken me quite a few years to reach the very top of my sport – and I have to confess that there have been times when I thought seriously about whether I made the right decision to take up snooker as a way of life. But over the years since I turned professional – and through the many years before that when I played as an amateur – I have had some wonderful moments which I hope I have been able to share with others.

There is no doubt in my mind that after winning, the most important aspect of any sport is knowing how to lose and to do so with dignity and good humour. Many find this increasingly difficult to cope with, as the pressures of professional snooker grow and the stakes get larger and larger.

Maybe it's because I'm Irish, because of the way I was brought up or because of the value I have had to put on life and on everything that happens to me and my family, but I have found that the ability to laugh at yourself and with others is the key to continual happiness.

I have put together in this book some of the stories and jokes that I have heard, been involved in and used during my travels round the world. Some are about myself, while others concern my fellow professionals. There are stories about referees and there are jokes from the commentary box.

As snooker takes us all round the world, inevitably we do a lot of travelling. You wouldn't believe some of the fun we get up to and I have therefore included just a few of the highlights over the years.

Quite a few of us professional snooker players find much of our relaxation on the golf course – and so I've included some amusing tales about us and the other green, both here and abroad.

Whatever else happens to me, I shall never forget – or, for that matter, be allowed to forget – that I am Irish. And from that point of view, no book on laughter would be complete without some Irish jokes. Like most of my fellow countrymen, I can put up with all the usual gags. I will, however, say just one thing about Irish jokes – the only people who can tell them properly are the Irish!

So here I go and I hope you are able to enjoy some of the amusement and laughter in these pages. I also hope that via the pages of this book I can, in a small way, put back some of the humour, fun and friendship that have meant so much to me through my snooker life – so far!

1. Early Days (and some very late nights)

WITH all the success that has come my way in the last year, never will I forget where my snooker all started, back in my home town of Coalisland. I received a tremendous welcome when I returned there after my world championship victory. It was a moment in my life I shall never forget.

I started playing the game in a small club called Jim Joe's, named after the owner, Jim Joe Gervin. He was quite a character, one of those people who viewed life very seriously and never consciously created humour out of a situation, but provided plenty of laughs nevertheless.

In the early days I played snooker regularly at the club and one evening I was about to play the black to clinch the frame against a friend of mine when Jim Joe walked past. He stopped behind me as I hit the shot and followed the black, which hung agonisingly over the lip of the pocket but refused to drop in.

As I got up from the table, he walked on past, muttering: "Be Jesus, that ball was away there, only it stopped."

Jim Joe and I were leaving his club one night – a particularly miserable evening – and stopped at the cloakroom area to pick up our coats. I went to get mine and put it on, waiting for Jim Joe to find his. He reached up to take the one remaining coat and, with the usual dry expression in his voice, said to me: "Would you believe it? Somebody's taken their coat and left me mine!"

Apart from running the club, Jim Joe was also in charge of the local football team. For the away matches, he organised a coach to take the team and some of the loyal supporters who followed the fortunes of the local lads. In order to get as many people on board as possible, Jim Joe brought a bench from the clubhouse and positioned it in the middle of the bus to provide more seating.

For those who are not familiar with Gaelic football, there are fifteen players on each side. The problem for Jim Joe was that every time he went to count up the number of players on the bus, to make sure nobody had been left behind, he always finished with fourteen – one short. In the team each week were the two O'Neill brothers and therein lay the problem.

Jim Joe would get out the team sheet and check the names off with those in the bus. He'd start off by saying: "Right. Well, McGhee's one and the two O'Neills's two, McGinty's three . . .". And so he continued, finally ending up with fourteen. And each time, he'd start recounting and each time he'd come up with fourteen. It took him a long time to realise where he was going wrong.

During my early snooker days I played in the local league, representing Jim Joe's of course. We had a pretty strong team and managed to see off most of the opposition. One particular evening we were due to play a club in a nearby town about four miles away. The club had only entered the league that season and this was our first visit.

When we arrived there, we were ushered into a small snooker room. Apart from commenting on its size, I also noticed the fire at the side of the table, which was blazing away. Alongside the fire was the cue rack, with a rather motley collection from which to choose.

I decided to give the table a quick try, and instead of getting my cue out of the case I went to the rack to try one of the club's. I picked out a cue that looked reasonable, but as I took hold of the butt to prepare for a shot at the balls on the table I felt the surface was rather rough. On closer inspection I saw that the butt end was all charred, and then it struck me. As well as using the cues on the table, somebody was also making sure that the fire was well stoked.

I must admit that this habit made it rather difficult to play reasonable snooker with the cues that the club provided, although the fire certainly appreciated the attention that was given to it by these improvised pokers.

When I came over to England looking for work, I had no particular plans to further my snooker career. But having played the odd game or two in some of the local clubs, I realised how good the standard of snooker had been at home. So I started showing more of an interest and got involved in local league snooker. This involved some travelling and, shortly after I found a job, I decided to buy a car. It was a Standard 10 and cost me the incredible sum of £15. It was a great little runner, even if I did have a few problems with the bodywork – and, in particular, the doors.

The front passenger door refused to open at all, while the rear doors would not shut. This meant tying them together inside with some rope to stop them flying open as I drove along. The only way in and out of the car was via the driver's door, which posed no problem for me but was a bit of a nuisance for any passengers.

I had arranged to pick up a member of our team for an away match and pulled up outside his house, giving him a couple of blasts on my horn, one of the few items on the car that actually worked. Eventually he appeared at the front door and came running down the steps to the car. He tried the front passenger door, fumbling away at the handle and dropping his cue case in the process. Then he went to the rear door and that wouldn't open either. By this stage he was getting rather frustrated

but, not wanting to appear stupid, walked round the back of the car and tried the other rear door. By now his temper was definitely getting the better of him, so I got out of the driver's seat and ushered him in.

What a performance that was, as he tried to clamber over my seat holding his precious cue case. Eventually he settled himself down in the front passenger seat, but it took quite a while for him to see the funny side as he cursed me and the car.

Before I turned professional I managed a snooker club in Preston for a while. Though I say it myself, I was by this stage getting quite useful at the game, so much so that I was seriously considering taking snooker up as a full-time occupation.

Every so often I would get the odd stranger walking into the club whom I could work out straight away was a hustler. This was something I never encouraged and I always tried to ensure that players like this never returned. Normally they were quite easy to spot, since they were big-headed and always had plenty to say for themselves.

On this occasion a nattily-dressed character swaggered in, carrying his cue case. It was early in the day and there were very few people about. First he asked where he could wash his hands and then, when he came back, he got his cue out of the case. Having looked around for a likely target and seeing nobody he felt was worth challenging, he turned to me and asked if I played the game. He obviously did not know me from Adam.

"Yes, I play a little bit," I replied, which was all he needed to take up the bait. So off we went to one of the tables.

We played three frames, in which I think he managed no more than six shots. To say he wasn't thrilled would be an understatement. He left the club a lot more quietly than he had come in and, strangely enough, I never saw him in there again!

There was quite a mixed bag of players in the club, including these scrap dealers who had almost certainly started off life as gipsies. One in particular was massive and I had got the word through that whenever there was some trouble around the town and he had had a few drinks, no fewer than ten policemen were called out to quieten him down.

In fact he was generally as good as gold when he came to my club, if a little scruffy. One day he came into the club and asked to use the best table, which I used to keep in top condition, mainly so that I could practise on it. I decided I didn't want to start any trouble by refusing him, so I gave him the balls and then politely suggested that I would be much happier if he would go and wash his hands first, since I didn't want the table to get all dirty.

He gave me a long, hard look, but I stood my ground and eventually he walked off to the cloakroom. I breathed a huge sigh of relief, because I really didn't think I would get away with it that easily.

Some while later I happened to glance over at the game and noticed this chap – all seventeen stone of him – lying across the table with his feet dangling over the side. Now the worst thing you can do is put all your weight on to the table, particularly since it is very easy to damage the cushion. So, without thinking, I switched off the light and shouted at him to get off the table.

From the snooker room there was a drop of about sixty feet to the ground from the windows. In my concern for the table, naturally I hadn't given this a moment's thought. There was a brief silence, then the chap got off the table, rested his cue and came over to me. He got within a few inches, stared at me for what seemed like an eternity, and then said: "Listen here, you red-headed * * * *. If you open your mouth just once more, you go straight out of the window."

I looked down a sheer drop and, deciding that discretion was the better part of valour, I let him carry on playing. Any damage to the table was preferable to that sixty-foot drop. I must have been terrified to think a heresy like that!

Sitting around in the club all day I used to get pretty bored at times – when I wasn't being threatened with violence, that is. Occasionally, for a bit of fun, I used to get out this weighted cue ball I had. The problem with a weighted ball is that it never runs in a straight line. Only a few people in the club knew about this and they were sworn to secrecy.

One day these two young lads came in. They were quite cocky and seemed to fancy their chances and I decided to have some fun with them. When they came over to book a table, I gave them my special cue ball to play with. They went over to one of the free tables and set up the balls. Not wishing to give the game away, I went over to another table and started knocking the balls around, glancing across every so often to see how they were getting on.

Every time they played a shot the cue ball went all over the place. At first they muttered some excuse to each other and then they started inspecting the cues. Eventually one of them gathered up the cues and brought them over to me.

"I'm sorry, but do you think you could swap these? I don't know what the matter is, but there's something definitely wrong with them." "I doubt it," I replied. "But by all means try some others if you want." And I

handed him another two cues. He took them back to the table, where the two were carefully inspected and the game continued.

The cue ball was still wandering all over the table and they just couldn't figure out what was wrong. After further deliberation, the other chap came over to me and asked if they could move over to the next table. I shrugged my shoulders and muttered that I would turn the other light on, desperately trying not to give the game away, since by this time I was near to bursting point.

Needless to say, they had no more luck on the other table and by this stage were totally bemused. I could see that they were on the verge of packing up, so I went over to them with an ordinary cue ball and said: "Try this one." They both gave me a very strange look, but finally took the other ball.

After a couple of shots it began to dawn on them what had happened. They exchanged bewildered glances, but then fortunately they both saw the funny side – otherwise I fear I would have been facing a sixty-foot drop from the window once again!

I had been living in Blackburn for some time and was working for a television company during the day and playing snooker in the evenings.

Alex Higgins had come over and I found him a small flat in Blackburn – and also fitted him up with a television.

We were playing quite a bit of snooker together, including the odd exhibition game locally, and I had been asked by a pensioners' club in the area if I would go there and put on a show for charity. I persuaded Alex to come with me.

I had warned him not to expect anything special and, sure enough, when we turned up on the afternoon in question he nearly had a fit when he saw the state of the table. But the room we were in was packed with pensioners, all sitting round expectantly, so there was no way we could say anything. They would have been very upset and bitterly disappointed otherwise.

So we started playing and the excitement built up around the room. After a quiet opening few shots, Alex, who has never been known for hitting the ball too gently, thumped this particular one very hard. The white flew off the table and landed at the feet of one of the elderly spectators in the front row.

Bearing in mind the table wasn't playing too well, I thought for a moment that this might have upset Alex. As I turned to look at him, I just caught a brief little smile on his face and sensed that he had made up his mind to have a little fun with the audience. The next thing I knew he was hitting the balls even harder and deliberately getting the white to fly off the table on to the laps of the men sitting at the front.

Fortunately even Alex's aim on this occasion was not as good as it might have been and none of the pensioners suffered any permanent damage, despite repeated attempts by Hurricane to play to the lap.

When I was first working for the television company, I ran round with various sets and other electrical appliances in this little old van. One day I was pulling up at a set of traffic lights when this car carved me up as it screeched to a halt. I felt pretty peeved about this, so I stuck my hand out of the window and stuffed two fingers up at the driver.

Unfortunately I hadn't timed my gesture particularly well, because there we were stuck in this line of traffic, with the lights on red, and this chap got out of his car. As he walked up to my van, I couldn't believe it. Trust me to pick the tallest man in Blackburn. He had to be all of six foot six, and big with it too.

He came right up to the driver's door and said: "So what's your game, then, sticking two fingers up at me like that?" Meanwhile the lights had changed back to green and everyone behind was wanting to get moving. They couldn't because our vehicles were in the way. So I plucked up courage and shouted back at the chap: "Now listen here. If you want to sort this out, just you pull in on the other side of the lights and I'll show you why I gave you two fingers."

The chap was quite pleased at the thought of getting stuck in properly and was obviously relishing a good punch-up – which is more than I could say of myself. All I could think of was how the hell I was going to get out of this mess. Meanwhile the chap jumped back in his car, roared across the lights and ran it on to the pavement on the other side. I started up my van and then watched to see where he was going. As soon as he had stopped again, I slammed my foot down and roared off past him as fast as I could. Mustering up even greater reserves of cowardice, I pulled a rude face and cocked my thumb up at him as I drove past.

I suppose I shouldn't have wound him up any more, because I spent the next half-hour chasing around the streets of Blackburn trying to shake him off. Fortunately I did finally manage to lose him, but it was tight.

My memories of the television company I once worked for were not all bad, I hasten to add. There were some pretty funny times too, particularly when short-wave radios were all the rage. We used to be inundated with Asians coming in to buy them. Apparently they were all trying to pick up home.

But the funniest occasion was when I happened to be in the shop and this Pakistani gentleman walked in. I looked up and asked if I could be of any help. "Oh yes, I do hope so. You see, I'm wanting to buy a brand-new second-hand television set."

Obviously my snooker fortunes have changed considerably over the years since I joined the professional ranks, but it is hard to forget the days when even the money for a game in the local club was hard to find. What we used to do was to play for the cost of the game and sometimes have a small side bet as well.

I was in my local club in Coalisland one night when a chap I knew fairly well and played quite regularly challenged me for the game and half-a-crown. He wasn't too bad a player, in fact, and the offer of a 40 start was pretty generous. It was therefore of no surprise when he eagerly accepted the handicap and I realised after I had committed myself that I needed to play very well to beat him.

He took the opening shot which, to my relief, left a couple of reds on. I went for a long pot and got it and was then able to build up a nice little break. Eventually it ended on 39. When I got up from the table, I turned to let my opponent back in. But he wasn't there.

He had obviously decided that, having lost his advantage, there was no way he could win the frame. Abandoning his cue, he had made his escape from the club room, leaving me to pay for the game.

Imagine my embarrassment. Not only did I have to fork out for the use of the table, which I could barely afford, but I also lost the chance of picking up an extra half-a-crown.

Inevitably we live much of our life out of a suitcase and visit all sorts of different hotels. I suppose there's a story behind every place I've been in, but one incident in a hotel in the Lake District I shall never forget. I had been doing a few shows for my local brewery – Matthew Brown – and this particular event was up in Workington. I was taken there by the promotions manager and we booked in at a hotel in Cockermouth, a few miles away. We were then shown our rooms and mine was really pokey. In fact it was so small that when you put the key in the door you broke the window.

Curious to know whether my friend from the brewery had fared any better, I wandered along the corridor to his room. When he opened the door I couldn't believe it, because he had been given the bridal suite with all the trimmings, including a four-poster bed. I thought to myself: that's nice. Here's me and I'm supposed to be the star attraction and the bloke from the brewery gets the best room in the hotel. I don't have to tell you what beer they sold in the bar. We got ready to leave for the evening's entertainment and, on our way through reception, told the girl that we would probably be back fairly late. In case they had all gone to bed, we asked if the front door could be left on the latch and our room keys on reception so that we didn't have to wake anyone up.

In fact it was well after two when we returned. We pulled up in the car park and walked over to the front door. It was locked. Obviously the girl had forgotten to pass on our message. We looked up at all the windows but the whole place was in darkness. There was no way we were going to spend the rest of the night in the car, so we went round to the back of the hotel to see if there was any other way in. Unfortunately this part of the building was surrounded by a high brick wall and the only access to the hotel was over the top. If that wasn't a daunting enough prospect, imagine climbing over wearing a dress suit and carrying a snooker cue. With the help of a leg-up, I managed to scale the wall and pull the brewery chap after me and, in pitch dark, we made our way to the back door. Fortunately this was open and we carefully fumbled our way through the kitchen, out into one of the corridors and eventually found the reception area.

We couldn't find a light switch anywhere, so I started groping about on the receptionist's desk for our keys. Of course, they weren't there. The girl had forgotten to leave those out too. Our only hope now was the manager's room, which I remembered was at the top of the first flight of stairs, quite near to our own bedrooms. We stumbled up the stairs and I paused outside the door. It was, by now, nearly three in the morning. Plucking up courage, I knocked hard. There was no answer and no movement. I knocked again. This time a dog started barking and then I heard somebody coughing away – a very wheasy cough. This was followed by some muttering, then the shuffle of footsteps and finally the door was opened.

I was confronted by this dishevelled-looking woman in her night-gown, blinking furiously as she peered out into the darkened corridor. When she finally managed to focus on us, she let out a little shriek of surprise, which was hardly surprising. Having been woken up in the middle of the night, the last thing you would expect to see was a chap in a dress suit carrying a cue case standing outside your bedroom door, though I suppose there are worse possibilities.

I was quite taken aback myself, but eventually muttered a few apologies and asked if we could have the keys to our rooms. Obviously too shocked – or sleepy – to enter into a discussion, she disappeared down the stairs and returned at lightning speed with two keys. I grabbed them and thanked her and we beat a hasty retreat in opposite directions to catch what was left of the night.

In helping the brewery with a range of promotional events, I would sometimes go to play in one of the clubs that stocked their beer. This was for them very much a public relations exercise, a way of saying thank you to their members.

On this occasion I was booked in to appear at one of the local clubs. It so happened that there was a big football match on the same evening, which was being televised. As we drove to the club, I jokingly commented that we'd be lucky to find a couple of people in – and they'd probably be more interested in playing snooker than watching it.

Many a true word is spoken in jest, as they say, and when we arrived at the club there were far less people than the brewery had hoped for. Still, we had come this far so there was no point in turning round and going home, so I agreed to stay and put on an exhibition.

On the table I was due to use, there were a couple of fellows already playing with furious concentration. So I got out my set of balls and my cue and waited patiently for them to finish. Unfortunately they were determined to complete their game and kept feeding money into the meter. Despite the blatant efforts of the club steward to get me on, they would not budge.

So I spent the next half-hour or so trying to pacify the chap from the brewery, who was getting more and more agitated by the minute, hopping from foot to foot. I must admit that it really didn't worry me and I was pleased to see the lads take their snooker so seriously. The only thing that bothered me was that the crowd left as soon as the two local lads had finished *their* game and didn't wait for my exhibition match. Some exhibition!

I was playing a lot of league matches shortly after I moved to Blackburn, but to begin with I had to travel on public transport since I hadn't yet reached the dizzy heights of being able to afford a car. The major problem with this was carrying my long metal cue case, particularly when the bus was crowded. I was then still playing with a one-piece cue.

Getting on the bus was bad enough, but deciding where to put the cue case was even more of a problem. Usually I tried to sit on the bench seat at the back of the bus, out of the way of the rest of the passengers. At least there I could stand the case up without it getting kicked over or knocked about by people getting on and off.

One evening I was off for a match and the bus was particularly crowded. Unfortunately the back seats were taken and I had to sit near the front by the gangway. So I squeezed in and propped my cue case up against my shoulder. At the next stop, this old lady got on, showed her pass and started walking down the bus to find a seat.

True to form, without waiting for her to sit down, the driver pulled away with his foot down and the bus lurched forward. The poor old lady stumbled and was about to fall. Instinctively she reached for one of the upright handrails, which to her utter horror started moving from side to side. She obviously thought the bus was about to collapse until she realised that what she had got hold of was not the handrail but my cue case.

As she fell on top of me, I have to admit that I was as bewildered as she was. In fact I was so embarrassed that I had no alternative but to offer her my seat, saying: "I didn't know you cared."

"Neither did I, dear," she said, "but for one moment I thought my luck had changed."

It's a little off-putting to find that you are not the person you thought you were – and the realisation can prove quite unnerving. This happened to me once at another club exhibition match organised by the Matthew Brown Brewery.

Shortly after I arrived one evening, this chap came up to me and explained that he would be refereeing for the evening and was anxious to reassure me that what he didn't know about the game of snooker and all the players wasn't worth knowing.

Safe in the knowledge that obviously this chap had the whole situation under control, we started playing. After the opening few shots, I managed the first score on the board by potting a red, followed by a black.

As he respotted the black, the referee called out: "Eight to Mr Brown."

I glanced over to him, trying to catch his attention, while the spectators started muttering among themselves. He took no notice and I decided not to say anything. He'd obviously made a mistake, probably because he was slightly nervous at the start of the match.

Shortly afterwards, my opponent went in off one of the colours. As the referee retrieved the cue ball he called out: "Four to Mr Brown."

This was all getting a little silly, so I thought I'd better check on the scoreboard to see what he had put up there. He was using the club board at the time and under the 'A' team he had put "versus Matthew Brown".

Above the scoreboard was this large banner which read "A Matthew Brown Sponsored Event".

At last the mystery was solved. Not only was I supporting the brewery, but that night I had become a member of the family as well!

2. Game for Anything

EVERYONE who has been involved in snooker over the years has stories to tell, whether about themselves or players of the past, in many cases handed down from generation to generation. When talking of snooker's characters over the years, how could you ever fail to mention the great Joe Davis, around whom the game as we know it has been built and developed.

Just as today, the players of the past used to play a lot of exhibition matches at different venues, some quite excellent and others very indifferent, to say the least. Apart from the state of the table itself, one of the major problems a snooker player faces is that of damp or humid conditions, since the balls never react in quite the way you want them to.

Joe Davis was booked in to play at a working man's club up in Cumbria. It was winter and the snow was falling heavily outside. The room in which he was due to play led straight off from the street and everyone coming in from outside brought the snow in by the bootful, trampling it into the floor as they walked to their seats. Before long, the air in the room was really humid and inevitably this affected the table and the way the balls ran.

As you can imagine for someone of his stature and ability, everything had to be just right for Joe when he was playing, but that was far from the case in this club. He suffered the conditions, nevertheless, in order to keep the audience happy. After all, there was little that could be done at this stage.

However, during one of the frames, he went up to a committee member sitting nearby. "This table I'm playing on, any chance of buying if off you?" The chap was, to say the least, surprised and couldn't believe his ears. The great Joe Davis wants to buy our table! he thought to himself. I can't believe it.

"Leave it with me, Joe," the chap told him and he went off to find the rest of the committee. During the interval they held a meeting, at which, of course, everyone agreed to let Joe have the table. To be quite honest, they would probably have been happy to give it to him, should he have suggested it.

So the chap went back to Joe. "Of course you can buy the table if you want. In fact, we would deem it a great privilege if you did. But we are slightly curious as to why you want it, Joe. Are you going to put it in your house, then?"

There was a brief silence, before Joe replied: "No, of course not. But I believe it's bonfire night next week and I'd love to burn the bloody thing!"

When you travel round playing at these clubs, you normally take with you a set of snooker balls, since you can never guarantee the quality of the ones there and a good set makes so much difference to how you play. Naturally all professional players take their own cues with them, as well.

Joe's younger brother, Fred, who also plays a bit, used to do quite a few exhibition matches with Rex Williams. On this occasion they had arrived at the club at which they had been booked to appear and were chatting away to the committee in the bar before the proceedings commenced.

Fred then decided he would like to take a look at the snooker room,

just to get an idea of the set-up before they went in. The secretary of the club happily agreed and showed him into the room that had been set aside. As Fred looked round, he saw the seating organised round the four walls which would probably take about 200 people. What struck him as rather odd, however, was that there was this large empty space in the middle and no table to be seen anywhere.

It seemed rather a daft question, but one Fred felt had to be asked. So he turned to the secretary: "Well, where's the table, then?"

The committee man looked rather surprised and replied: "Oh! Don't you normally bring one with you?"

Much to the embarrassment of the club – and the understandable irritation of all those who had come to watch – there was no table to play on and, since it takes a good four or five hours to set one up, no chance of getting one in time.

Without doubt some of the strangest places to play snooker in are the holiday camps, although in fairness some of them do provide good tables – and particularly for major tournaments. As with everything else, there are notable exceptions and often you have to put up with some pretty awful conditions.

Although cushions are designed specifically to enable you to bounce the balls off them, I have come across many tables where they are there purely and simply to stop the balls falling off!

Wherever you go, you will always find somebody there who is desperate to get involved and offers to help in any way possible. It could be anyone, from the cleaning staff to somebody in the kitchens.

Poor David Taylor had a terrible experience at one camp, after he had been pestered for ages by this chap insisting that there must be something he could do for him. Eventually David gave in: "Well, there's just one thing I would be grateful if you could check on. I'm coming in tomorrow to play this exhibition match and I would appreciate it if the table was properly brushed ready. Could you manage to do that?"

"Of course," the chap replied. "I'll brush the table for you, Mr Taylor."

David hadn't the faintest idea whether this chap knew anything about snooker tables. He assumed he must, since he hadn't asked him how it was done. However, whatever misgivings he may have had could never have matched what he saw the next day, as he passed the snooker room on his way to get a cup of coffee. He was due to play shortly and decided to pop his head round the door to check that everything was all right.

To his horror and utter disbelief, he saw the chap walking across the table with this great big broom, whistling away to himself as he swept the cloth. David quickly changed his mind about the coffee and went off to get a stiff drink from the bar.

Tables are always a bone of contention, since the way they play can make such a big difference to a snooker player's game. This is always a problem when you travel round to different venues doing exhibition matches, particularly where the local club officials look after and prepare the table.

One of the worst conditions for a snooker table is dampness or humidity, since any moisture can have a marked effect on how the cloth reacts.

I was playing an exhibition match in a club in the Blackburn area and when I arrived one of the officials came straight up to me and announced with great satisfaction and obvious pride: "You'll be OK tonight, Mr Taylor. The table is in first-class condition and I know you're going to like it."

"Oh," I replied, with an obvious note of suspicion, not to say apprehension. "Why's that?"

"Because I washed it for you specially this afternoon."

He wasn't joking, either. When I got to the table, the cloth was absolutely saturated.

As far as choice of cues is concerned, the two-piece ones are definitely the most popular now – and the main reason for this is that they are so much more convenient to carry around. They do, however, have their drawbacks, as I was to find out on one trip to the Channel Islands.

Shortly after I changed from the traditional one-piece cue, I was travelling to Jersey and had got off the plane with my hand luggage, which included my diminutive cue case. I was walking out, having cleared customs, when these two security officers descended on me.

I was terrified. Although I knew I had nothing to fear, since I wasn't trying to sneak anything through, for one awful moment I wondered whether they were going to pull me in or whether perhaps someone had planted something on me without my knowing. While all this was going through my mind, the two men had come right up to me. I was shaking like a leaf, which could have made matters worse.

One of them then spoke up: "We've just had a bet between ourselves as to what's in that small case you're carrying." I couldn't believe it. There was only my cue in there . . . or was there?

He went on: "I said it was a cue, but my colleague thinks it's a large mouth organ!"

I burst out laughing, more from relief than anything else. They looked at me rather bemused, not realising why I found the matter so funny. I didn't bother to explain, but eagerly opened the case and hurried on my way, leaving them to sort out payment for the wager.

We've all, I'm sure, lived through those awful moments when we've dropped the most almighty clanger and have just stood there and prayed that the ground would open and swallow us up.

One of the worst occasions for me, believe it or not, was beside a snooker table. Where else, you may ask? I was playing this chap in a club, while the rest of the party were seated at a nearby table chatting. Earlier that day we had been round the golf course together and I had previously met him on several occasions with someone I naturally presumed was his wife.

He was in the middle of a reasonable break when I asked him: "Where's the wife tonight?" He pointed across to the nearby table. I didn't want to appear rude, so when we had finished that frame and the balls were being set up for the next one, I decided to wander over and say hello. So I went up to this lady with blonde hair, gave her a quick kiss and said: "Nice to see you again." She looked at me very strangely and then turned to the man sitting next to her, who was staring very suspiciously at both of us.

It was then that it hit me. The chap sitting next to her was obviously her husband – or at least, she was certainly not the wife of the fellow I was playing with. Immediately I went bright red. Glancing quickly

round the table, I then realised who this fellow's wife really was and said, with acute embarrassment: "Oh, you've changed your hair style." I couldn't think of anything better to say on the spur of the moment.

I suspect the blonde lady realised my predicament, for she replied immediately: "Yes, in fact I have." I smiled and quickly returned to the snooker table.

That little episode certainly did little for my game and for a while it was impossible to concentrate. Then, about halfway through the frame, I just collapsed over the table laughing. I got some pretty strange looks after that, I can tell you, but I never let on the reason for that sudden outburst and to this day nobody watching us knew what I was laughing about – except possibly the two ladies concerned.

It's strange in a way how you can feel as embarrassed for others as you can for yourself and certainly this is how I felt after one awful moment while I was playing Bill Werbeniuk in the Champion of Champions tournament a few years back.

Bill, as all followers of the game will know, is quite a big fellow. During our match, he went to play a shot for which he had to get himself partly on to the table. As he bent over to hit the ball, there was this loud ripping sound. Immediately he got off the table, muttered something inaudible and rushed out of the hall.

Poor Bill. He had only split his trousers right up the back. I suppose that wouldn't have been too bad, except that he never wears any under-pants!

The match was held up while we all waited expectantly for what must have been one of the most embarrassing returns for anyone to the table. Having had a quick stitch job done to close up the gap, to his eternal credit he simply walked straight up to the table and took his shot as though nothing had happened. He was given a great round of applause after that performance.

I shall never forget the first time I met Steve Davis in a final. It was at one of the Romford Pro-Am tournaments and just before Steve turned pro-fessional. Of course Steve lived on the tables at Romford and obviously

knew this one back to front. He proceeded to beat me 8–0, much to the delight of the home supporters.

I wouldn't have minded quite so much, except that the final happened to coincide with my birthday. As I was contemplating my defeat, I had to admit it wasn't the best way to be celebrating it.

But all was not lost, because Barry Hearn – Steve's manager and now mine, of course – had organised a pleasant surprise, a huge birthday cake which was presented to me afterwards. And when I went to blow out the candles, the whole crowd started singing 'For He's a Jolly Good Fellow' at the top of their voices. No wonder they were generous. I'd just been beaten by the local hero.

We used to play a fair amount of Pro-Celebrity snooker on television, before the advent of all the professional tournaments we have now, most of which are covered by either BBC or ITV. In this particular match I was paired with Kenny Lynch against Graham Miles and Les Dawson.

Although now even a televised maximum break seems almost commonplace, in those days a century break on the television was quite an event and yours truly, despite all the efforts of the opposition, was on the verge of achieving just that. In fact I had reached 95 and was going well. Les Dawson, who had barracked me the whole way through and never stopped talking, wasn't going to change his tactics now – and in fairness there was no reason why he should have understood the importance of this achievement.

While the rest of the players and the whole of the audience went absolutely quiet, sensing I was about to complete the century break, Les was preparing himself for his next quip. As I stretched across the table to cut in this particularly tricky red and was about to play the shot, Les shouted out: "Your flies are open." Immediately the crowd burst out laughing and I collapsed on the table.

Not only was I determined, after this interruption, to make the 100 break but I also decided to play the joke right through. So I got up from the table, covering my vital parts as best I could, and left the hall, returning minutes later with a different pair of trousers on. I then went up to the table and, using the rest this time, potted the red. Amid tremendous applause, I went on to make a break of 125.

Whether I owed that triumph to Les or the new pair of trousers, I have never quite been able to decide.

Les Dawson is a great character with a particularly quick and accurate wit, and always provides excellent entertainment. In fact it was in the same match that he almost brought the house down, although I am pleased to say that this time it was not at my expense.

Kenny Lynch, my partner, was at the table and had done exceptionally well to pot a very difficult red, leaving himself an easy black right over the pocket. After some seconds carefully studying the ball, he got down to play the shot. As he brought his cue back, Les said to him softly but loud enough for everyone to hear: "Kenny, I wouldn't pot that if I were you. It might be a relative."

I had considerable success in the Pro-Celebrity tournaments, winning three times with Bill Maynard as my partner. On one occasion we were matched against David Taylor and the Liverpool comedian Mike Burton.

As I am sure Mike would be the first to admit, he wasn't too hot at the game, but with his crew-cut hair style and wearing large glasses rather like mine, I have to say he looked pretty impressive.

Realising Mike's limitations on the snooker table, David spent a fair bit of time advising him on the type of shot to play. This time, as Mike got down to play, David leant over him and said: "Play a semi-stun shot for this one, Mike."

Mike got up from the table and looked at his partner in total bewilderment. "What's a semi-stun shot, for Christ's sake?"

Before David could explain, Bill Maynard chipped in: "Quite simple, really. If you miss the red, he'll hit you over the head with the cue!"

In the last two or three years my glasses have inevitably become my trademark and I am always getting plenty of stick over them. The truth of the matter is that players who need glasses can be at a distinct disadvantage when the head is down over the table and you're looking up and along the line of the shot. My upside-down design is therefore ideal since it gives me plenty of lens above the eye, rather than below it.

A few years back, there was a chap in Manchester who played a lot of challenge matches for money. On this particular occasion a match had been arranged with this opponent who he had never seen play but had been told a lot about. The purse was £1,000.

When the two met at the club to play, the opponent was wearing one of the thickest pairs of bifocals you have ever seen. "This is going to be the easiest £1,000 I've ever made," the other thought to himself.

Then the match got under way. They were due to play the best of nine frames but it never looked like going the distance as the bespectacled challenger played like a man possessed. He potted everything in sight and couldn't miss a ball, ending up winning in five straight frames.

The other chap couldn't believe his eyes, but was so full of admiration for his opponent that after it was all over he went up and shook him generously by the hand. "Well, that's amazing. How on earth do you manage to play like that when you're wearing glasses – and bifocals at that?"

The fellow looked at him: "It's quite simple, really. Because I've got bifocals, when I get down to take a shot I see two balls – one big one and one little one. And as I look along the line of the shot I see two pockets – one big one and one little one."

"But I don't understand. How does that make things easier?"

"Well, I simply pot the little ball into the big pocket."

The other chap was dumbfounded by this and went away thinking to himself: "Hmm. I think I'll try a pair of those bifocals." So he went and bought himself a pair and started practising. After a few weeks he offered the same guy another challenge match and turned up wearing an identical pair of glasses.

Just before he was about to make the opening break, he had an urgent call of nature and disappeared into the cloakroom. When he came back his opponent couldn't help but notice that his right trouser leg was soaking wet.

"What's the problem? Did you have an accident?"

"Not exactly. I went in to relieve myself, undid my flies and pulled it out. As I looked down, I saw a big one and a little one. I thought: that can't be mine and put it back again!"

The 1984–85 season was a great one for me, highlighted of course by winning the World Championship for the first time. The closest I had come before was in 1979, when I literally had the trophy in my reach. That year I was beaten by Terry Griffiths in the final, a great achievement for him since he had only turned professional that season.

Having seen off the challenge of Steve Davis and Ray Reardon, by the time I got to the final I was a firm favourite to take the title. Even after the first day's play, when we were level at fifteen frames apiece, I was confident that this was to be my year. Terry had other ideas and gradually pulled ahead to win.

In those days, the two finalists were the guests of the sponsors, Embassy, after the match and were wined and dined along with their wives. When the presentations and interviews were over, I went back to the dressing room to change. Then came a knock on the door. It was Terry. I must admit that at that stage I did not know him particularly well, and I was unaware that he had no car. In fact he had come to ask me if I would give him and his wife, Annette, a lift to the restaurant.

Naturally I agreed and we met in the car park. You can imagine how I felt seeing him there holding the trophy and having to load it into the boot of my car. So there I was, driving through Sheffield with the world champion and – in the back – the trophy that I so nearly claimed for myself.

The next time it found its way into the boot of my car, I am pleased to say that it was mine by right – for a year, at least.

Another time with Terry I remember is after we had finished an exhibition match in Tunbridge Wells. We retired to our hotel fairly promptly, since we had to be up at the crack of dawn the next day to head north. We managed to get up at about five o'clock and were soon on our way, making sure we missed all the traffic going through London.

When we got to London, the traffic was chock-a-block. I think there must have been an accident or something, because we sat in this jam for ages. Terry was behind me in his new car, getting more and more impatient. When the traffic started to move forward a little, Terry called out that he knew a short cut. So I waved him on and followed.

On the way we came up to this set of traffic lights, which was in the middle of changing to red. Terry, of course, put his foot down and raced through. Since the traffic was pretty heavy all round and I didn't want to lose him, I went to do the same thing. Unfortunately by the time I crossed over, the lights had turned to red, and I saw this young policeman step out from the pavement and flag me down. There was nothing I could do about it except pull up. If not I would either have had to run him over or swerve and hit the oncoming traffic. So while Terry was racing on ahead, there was I being booked by this young policeman – and on foot, of all things. "Who do you think you are – Hurricane Higgins?" he said.

Finally I was able to get away, but by this time I had lost Terry completely. I didn't know where he had gone and had to find my own way to the M1. I eventually met up with him in the first service station. When I walked in to have a coffee and some breakfast, there was Terry sitting looking at me from the corner, choking with laughter over a bacon sandwich.

Terry Griffiths, who certainly doesn't need to ask me for a lift anymore!

I must admit, with the thought of an endorsement weighing heavily on my mind, I'm afraid I had a job seeing the funny side of that little episode.

3. Making an Exhibition of Myself

A large part of a snooker professional's life is taken up with playing exhibition matches and these can be a lot of fun. Although we do play a fair amount of snooker seriously, there are times when you can – and in fact are expected to – entertain the crowd. These sessions get very light-hearted and there's always plenty of banter with members of the audience.

There's always one or two who enjoy giving you a bit of stick from time to time and I don't mind this at all, since it gives you the chance to get back at them and start what can be quite an amusing exchange.

Once in a while it does get a little out of hand and I remember on one occasion having a particular amount of bother from a tired and emotional gentleman who wouldn't stop talking and was obviously starting to spoil others' enjoyment. So I turned to the audience and said: "You'll have to excuse him. He's the only fellow I know who can put three balls in his mouth and not get a cannon!"

Everyone fell about at this and, I am pleased to say, we never got another peep out of the fellow.

After we have played a few frames in an exhibition match, we move on to some trick shots and as a finale I try the one where you get somebody to lie on the table and then attempt to pot the black ball from out of their mouth. It's one of the most risky shots to attempt but it's great when it works.

When I was playing with Terry Griffiths at Tunbridge Wells we had drawn a good crowd – about twelve hundred people. We were getting to the end of the show and I decided to try this particular trick with Terry. So I got him to lie on the table and take a block of chalk in his mouth. The secret is to bite it with your teeth, but making sure it sits up as high as possible in the mouth. I then put another block of chalk on the cushion in line with Terry's mouth and the pocket and placed the black ball in his mouth and the white ball on the cushion.

The place went quiet as I lined up for the shot. The first attempt failed, as did the second and third, and I could sense the people in the audience getting a little restless. When was he going to pot the black, they were obviously thinking to themselves.

Because of the size of the hall, both Terry and I were wearing radio mikes so that everyone could hear what we were saying. After the third attempt, Terry got up from the table and said to me: "Why don't we swop over. You get on the table and I'll try to pot the black." I was reluctant to do this and admit defeat, but finally I agreed. Strangely enough, it was the first time I had been the 'stooge' for this trick.

Terry set the balls up and got ready to play the cue ball. Then he started giggling. Terry is quite prone to this and when he does it you find yourself joining in, since it is very infectious. Because he had his mike on, everyone heard and eventually joined in. I took the ball and chalk out of my mouth and said to him: "What are you laughing about?"

"Well," he said, "I've never played this shot before, actually."

I thought he must be joking, so I got back down on the table and he set the black up again. Down he got to play the white and at his first attempt he managed to hit me smack on the jaw. With the mike amplifying the sound of this contact, the people in the audience thought he had broken it, since there was a sickening crack.

I'm pleased to say that nothing was broken, although my jaw was sore for quite a while afterwards. Needless to say, I didn't let him have another try.

I was playing the same trick shot at the Leisure Centre in Kingston some while later when I enjoyed one of those amusing moments that crop up quite by chance. Again there was a good crowd, about six hundred people this time, and I was having a fair bit of banter with this chap in the

audience. He was a great character – a little cockney in his mid-sixties, I should say – and everyone was loving the performance.

I decided to pull him out and bring him down for this trick, much to his surprise and the crowd's amusement. So I got him to lie on the table and gave him a block of chalk. "Just bite into this," I told him. But he just lay there, looking at me rather puzzled. "What's the problem?" "Well, I ain't got no teeth." And he opened his mouth wide. Sure enough, he was right. Everyone roared with laughter.

"Oh well, we'll have to improvise this one," I said. "Can you suck on the chalk instead?" So he did and I managed to balance the black ball, which was sitting well down in this valley between his nose and his chin. The prospects of playing the shot successfully looked pretty remote and my main concern was not to whack him on the jaw. I knew from bitter experience how painful that could be! But having gone this far and got him on the table, I wasn't going to give in now.

I shall never know to this day how I managed it, but somehow I hit the shot just right and managed to dig the black out of his mouth and send it straight into the pocket. There was a great applause all round and, much relieved, the chap returned to his seat unscathed.

When playing the trick shot with the black in someone's mouth, I have sometimes called down a lady to help me with the trick. On one occasion I noticed this delightful blonde sitting near the front of the hall and finally persuaded her to give me a hand.

First I asked her to lie on the table, which brought some predictable comments from the male sections of the audience. She was particularly nervous and as she lay there with the block of chalk in her mouth and the black ball balanced on top, I turned to the crowd and said: "Right, ladies and gentlemen. Now we have to turn off all the lights." This brought a noisy round of applause.

"Please," I said, "you must keep as quiet as you can while I attempt the trick. Both I and my delightful partner need complete hush so as not to upset our concentration. The last time I attempted this, the lady in question swallowed the black." The audience burst out laughing again.

As they quietened down, I added: "And you should have seen the shot I had to play to get the black out again."

The best moment I had with a trick shot was over in Northern Ireland. I was playing an exhibition match at Inniskillin in a place called The Forum. The people there had arranged for this chap to challenge me to a frame. He turned out to be a super character, although he wasn't quite all there and had the mickey taken out of him something rotten. The lads had dressed him up for the occasion and he appeared in a dress-suit, which must have been all of forty years old, complete with bow tie and a hankie in his top pocket.

The balls were set up on the table and I took the opening shot. Then I offered him the table and he walked up, still with his jacket on, to take his shot. I've got a tough match on here, I thought to myself. Anyway, I tried to set him up with as many shots as I could and eventually he managed to pot a couple of reds, which naturally brought the house down. He was a really good sport and the crowd were loving it.

After this frame, I went on to play some trick shots, including the one with the pyramid of reds. For those of you who are not familiar with this one, I will explain.

You first set up the pyramid and then take out one of the reds. The triangle is then laid on the table with one of the points near the pink spot and the white is sited there with the triangle resting on it. The idea is to play the red you have taken out off three cushions and back to flick the white out of the way, so that the triangle drops down on the cloth with the remaining red inside with the other fourteen.

Not the easiest of shots, I can tell you. Well, I tried it three times and just couldn't get it to work. Then the crowd started shouting for this chap I had just played to be given a chance. Not wanting to spoil everyone's fun I agreed, since although I knew he didn't have a cat's chance of doing it at least it would provide plenty of amusement. So on came Willie 'Speedway' Watson, I think they called him. The poor fellow didn't quite know what was happening, but he took his cue out of the case again and approached the table.

Although I still had serious reservations about the wisdom of all this, I thought I couldn't stop now and send him back. So, bearing in mind he could hardly play the game, I decided I would have to give him some help. I even lent him my cue, which is very unusual. Normally a good player will never let anyone else use his own special cue.

Having set up the balls and the triangle, I walked round the table and pointed with my finger to where on the cushion he needed to hit the red ball in order to effect the trick. He stood there trying to work it all out and I realised there was no way he was going to hit the cushion in the right place, let alone send it on round the table. We're right in trouble here, I thought.

So I went back round the table and got behind him. While he got down and took up his bridge position with the left hand, I held the butt of the cue to direct the shot, all the time thinking to myself: there's no way he's going to get this.

We struck the ball which, to my utter amazement, went like a dream, off the first cushion, then the second and third and came back, flicking the white out of the way as the triangle fell down over the fifteen reds. It was a miracle.

Although I don't think Speedway quite realised what he had done, the place erupted and he was given the loudest cheer of the night. It was quite a sight – Speedway smiling all over his face, bowing to the audience which was as delighted as he was.

It never bothers me if I lose the odd game when playing exhibitions. Not only does it add more interest for the audience, but equally it does the world of good for the ego of the club player involved.

One of the most comprehensive defeats I have suffered was at a club in Sunderland quite a few years ago against a chap probably three times my age, since he was getting on for seventy. I found out afterwards that he used to play professional football and was a former goalkeeper for Sunderland.

I was going through the frames with different people from the club when he came out to the table. He was given a tremendous reception and I realised straight away that he was certainly a man to be respected.

He was wearing a cloth cap and had his jacket on – neither of which he removed.

As usual, I broke and smashed the pack of reds all over the place just to give him an opening. That was my first and fatal mistake. He stepped in and carefully built up a break of 65. That set everyone going. I went back on the table with one red left, which I missed. Back he came, potted the last red and proceeded to clear up all the colours. So there I was, without a score, and he'd beaten me by something like 95 points. I don't have to tell you that this brought the house down and he was given a wonderful reception as he returned to his seat.

The balls were set up again for the next player. In the meantime, I walked over to where he was sitting, took his cap off his head and put it on mine, as much as to say: well, if it works for you, maybe it'll work for me.

The crowd were delighted, honour was satisfied and the old boy smiled at me appreciatively.

Playing exhibition matches does tend to land you in the most extraordinary situations, but I doubt if any could match the experience Willie Thorne and I went through when we agreed to put on a show in the Shetlands. Yes, believe it or not, they have heard of snooker that far north.

We were playing in the Jameson's at the time, but neither Willie nor I were due to play again for a few days and so we accepted an invitation from some snooker buffs on the island. This involved travelling from Newcastle to Aberdeen and then picking up a flight from there. Although the plans were fairly complicated, we were confident of getting there and back without too much trouble. By flying out on Thursday to play that night, we would return on the Friday. In any case, Willie wasn't due to reappear until the Sunday.

When we arrived at Aberdeen, we transferred to a light aircraft which took us on to the island. During the flight we got chatting to the pilot, who told us that in the six years he had been doing that run he hadn't experienced any delays worth worrying about. Anyway, there were two airfields on the island and even if one were closed, you could normally get away from the other one. Since we had been slightly apprehensive about the fact that we could end up stranded and not be able to get back in time to play our next matches in the Jameson, we both felt a little better at hearing this.

The exhibition was a great success and we returned to our hotel bedrooms and booked in an early call for the following morning. When we were woken, the first thing we did was to draw the curtains and check on the weather. We couldn't believe it. The cloud was so thick you couldn't see across the street. We dressed quickly and went down to take a look outside. By now the weather was so bad you could barely see your finger in front of you.

After a hasty breakfast, we packed and got a car to the airfield, where we waited anxiously for news of any flights out. Since no planes had flown in that morning there was nothing to board, let alone fly out in. The hours ticked past and Willie, in particular, was beginning to panic. In the end, having persuaded him that there was no immediate problem and that the weather was bound to have cleared by the morning, we returned to the hotel and booked in for a second night.

Unfortunately there was little change in the conditions when we got up the following day and, with visions of a repeat of the day before, Willie

was now in quite a state, muttering how he doubted we'd ever get off the wretched island. Then he rushed to the phone and started ringing round to see if there was a private plane available to take us back to the mainland.

Willie Thorne, shell-shocked after paying our cab fare from Aberdeen to Newcastle.

Willie finally managed to locate a pilot who was prepared to fly us out and with a considerable amount of relief we boarded this plane. We had with us a fitter who had come to set up the table correctly, but because the plane was so small he was rather unceremoniously bundled into the tail end, along with his tool bag.

Amazingly enough it proved to be one of the best flights I have been on. Sitting in this tiny plane looking down on the scenery below was rather like watching those old war films – without the German fighters, of course.

It was late Saturday evening when we finally touched down at Aberdeen. We had missed the last train to Newcastle and didn't have time to stay the night since Willie was due to play the following morning. Our only hope was to grab a taxi. So Willie headed for the cab rank outside the airport building and, as I appeared, he was being surrounded by cabbies, who had obviously recognised him and were all vying for the fare.

By the time I reached him, there was only one cabbie left. When I asked him what the score was, he said: "It was fine till I told them we didn't want to get into town but had to go to Newcastle." Fortunately the one that was left was a bigger snooker fan than the rest of them and, despite the fact that he had been on duty all day, he agreed to take us when we explained our predicament. Poor fellow! He had a ten-hour round trip ahead of him.

It was at this stage that I made one of the smartest moves of my life. Having loaded our luggage into the boot, I went and sat in the back seat. Fortunately Willie prefers travelling in the front anyway because he finds it more comfortable, so he made no objection. What he hadn't bargained for was the fact that the cabbie talked non-stop for the whole of the journey. As I lay back and slept most of the way, Willie had to sit there and keep saying: "Yes" and "No". He admitted afterwards that he hadn't understood a word of what the chap was saying!

When we finally arrived at our hotel in Newcastle, I was reasonably refreshed after my nap. Poor Willie, on the other hand, hadn't had a wink of sleep and was absolutely shattered.

I must say it was quite an experience, our little excursion to the Shetlands. But what hurt us more than anything was the fact that although we had been well paid for the exhibition, we had to fork out

£750 for the plane and another £150 for the taxi. Needless to say we ended up well out of pocket.

Even though as professionals we get very used to performing in front of large crowds, it can be fairly nerve-racking to be standing centre-stage, with all those eyes focused upon you, watching your every movement. Although I have over the years got used to this situation, there is always the odd occasion when something happens to throw you completely. And it seems to occur in the unlikeliest of situations.

I was playing an exhibition match at a working men's club in the North-East, a superb place with all the facilities. But it soon became obvious that they were not used to staging this type of event. The kind of hospitality you receive does, of course, vary from place to place and it is always interesting to see how different people cope with it.

Usually with an exhibition, I arrange to play four frames and then take a break before continuing to the end of the evening. Sometimes you are positively overwhelmed by the generosity of your hosts and have to refuse politely the refreshments they offer. At other times, you may not even be given a cup of coffee.

This particular evening I had just finished the fourth frame and looked around to see whether anyone was coming to invite me out of the games room for a quick break. Then I noticed a chap coming towards me with a small package in his hand. It was covered in tin-foil and looked very much like somebody's lunch pack. As I was putting my jacket on, he stuffed what turned out to be a pile of egg and cress sandwiches into my hand and waited, presumably for some acknowledgement or expression of gratitude.

So there I was, stood in the middle of this room which was crowded with spectators, with my dress suit on holding a pack of sandwiches. It wouldn't have surprised me if he had suggested I eat them over the snooker table. What could I do? I didn't want to appear rude or ungrateful. On the other hand, there was no way I was going to tuck into the sandwiches in front of all those people. Now if it had been smoked salmon it would have been a different matter!

"Thank you," I said. "Actually I'm not that hungry at the moment, but I'll keep them for later." He nodded his approval and left. With that I

slipped them quickly under the table, where they remained until the cleaners arrived the next morning. At least, I think that's who removed them – Alex Higgins always has a lean and hungry look, though!

4. Cue for a Joke

IT'S often very difficult when you are putting on an exhibition in a club to get the people warmed up sufficiently. I always try to get them on my side from the start and the easiest way to do this is to tell a few stories. Ideally these need to be about fellow players – and certainly this is what audiences are expecting. So, in the hope that my colleagues will forgive me repeating some of them, I include here just a few.

Big Bill Werbeniuk is one of the game's great characters and, as probably most people who follow snooker know, he does like a pint or two of lager before he plays – and a few more during the match. On one particular occasion he got through no less than twenty pints, which is normally no problem. Unfortunately he had made the mistake, because he was feeling a little peckish, of eating a dozen packets of peanuts as well. On the way back to his hotel that evening, he accidentally passed wind and pebble-dashed four houses.

I was telling this story in a club one night and when I had finished there was the usual round of laughter. Then I heard this little lad, who could only have been five or six, turn to his father and say: "Dad, what does pebbledash mean?" The place erupted.

Alex Higgins always has plenty of supporters, even when he's not playing. Before I started one particular show, therefore, I asked the crowd:

Big Bill Webeniuk, a great character in every sense.

"Are there any Alex Higgins supporters in tonight?" There was a great cheer from different parts of the hall.

"Well, I'm afraid you're a bit unlucky tonight," I went on. "Alex should have been here, but he was launching a ship in Belfast today. He hasn't turned up yet and I understand that they are still trying to get him to let go of the bottle."

Incidentally, a lot of people have asked me why Alex doesn't use a two-piece cue. Well, the reason is that he did try one out about five years ago. He had to abandon it when he lost the book of instructions.

Steve Davis, as we all know, has been very successful at snooker in the last few years and I am often quizzed as to how much he has actually earned from the game during this time. I have to admit I have no idea, except to say that he wrote out a cheque recently and the bank bounced.

But if you think that Steve has got plenty of money, you ought to talk to his manager, Barry Hearn. When I found out what he earns the other day, I couldn't believe it. Barry's the only man I know who keeps Swiss money in English banks.

The South African Perrie Mans was due to appear in a televised tournament some years ago and was messing about on the table during rehearsals before the actual event. When he spotted the referee, he went up to him.

"About tonight," he said, "what are we supposed to be wearing? Presumably we don't have to put on dress-suits for this." The referee nodded his head. "You mean to say we can't come on in lounge suits? Well, that's ridiculous."

Then an argument ensued, since Perrie was determined to get his money's worth out of this chap. Finally the referee had had enough. "Now look," he said to Perrie, "protocol says you should wear a dress-suit and that's all there is to it!"

Perrie pretended to get really angry at this and he turned to his partner, who happened to be the luckless Eddie Charlton. "Who the hell's this guy Protocol, anyway? And what's he got to do with the tournament?"

The referee stood there speechless, while Perrie stormed off to get changed.

*Perrie Mans, who once challenged protocol and Eddie Charlton
at the same time and lived to tell the tale.*

Graham Miles, as I have said, spends much of his time confusing every-one around him. He's one of those people who, if there are only two items on the menu, will take half-an-hour deciding which one to have. The trouble is that he knows what he wants but wastes all that time thinking about what the other one might be like.

A group of us were playing up in Edinburgh and happened to stop at this restaurant one evening. We were shown to a table and then passed the menus. We managed to sort out the important part – ordering the wine – without too much trouble, but then it came to the food. When the waiter got round to taking Graham's order, Graham said to him: "What's the soup of the day?" The waiter replied: "Twenty-five pence, sir."

Graham scowled at the waiter and continued with the rest of his order.

We came to the end of the meal without too many problems or dramas, and two of us ordered up coffee. Now Graham likes to think he's a bit of a coffee connoisseur, pouring the cream in over a spoon and so on. So you should have seen his face when the waiter returned a few minutes later carrying two cups of coffee which looked all greasy.

"Did you try pouring in the cream carefully over the back of a spoon?" he asked the waiter. "Yes sir, I did." The poor man was sent back to the kitchen to fetch two more coffees. Graham had volunteered to add the cream just to show the waiter how it should be done properly.

The waiter finally returned carrying two cups of black coffee and two cartons of cream. Graham asked for a spoon and took one of the triangular cartons, which he opened. Then with the upturned spoon poised over the top of the coffee, he carefully tipped up the cream. Unfortunately nothing came out, so he started to squeeze the carton instead.

By now we were all watching this performance, including the waiter who was desperately trying to hide a broad grin. The next thing Graham knew was that a large blob of cream had shot out of the carton and plopped straight in the coffee, splashing it over the sides of the cup and on to his trousers.

Poor Graham. He couldn't look at the waiter, who by now was beating a tactful retreat from the table.

For those who don't know, Ray Reardon is known affectionately as Dracula, although I shall leave you to work out the reason why. He's not

had the easiest of times over the last few years, but certainly he showed some of his old skills and guile during the 1985 World Championships, when he reached the semi-finals.

I eventually discovered from Ray why this was. He had just returned from a six-week refresher course in Trannsylvania, where he'd really got his teeth stuck into things.

5. Return Matches

OVER the years, I have tried to take as many of my fellow professionals back over to Northern Ireland with me, since I feel I owe it to all the fans – and particularly to my own supporters – to show them as much top snooker as I can.

On one occasion Terry Griffiths agreed to come with me and we ended up in my local club. Since the people there had all seen my trick shots many times, I thought it would be nice to let Terry do some of his own instead. He went down very well with everyone. The crowd liked him a lot, particularly his soft Welsh accent.

A very popular trick which everyone enjoys watching is the machine-gun shot. This is, as the name suggests, a rapid-fire shot where you play the white ball towards the pocket and try to fire in a number of reds before it gets there.

So Terry decided to use this as his finale and set the balls up ready. He then turned to the audience: "Well, ladies and gentlemen, to finish off I am going to attempt the famous machine-gun shot." He paused, then went on: "The only trouble is that I haven't got a machine-gun." At which a voice from the back of the audience called out: "Don't you worry, Terry. We can soon fix that up for you!"

While we were out in Northern Ireland, Terry insisted that I took him to Belfast, since he wanted to see for himself how bad the trouble really was there. The strange thing is that most people who visit the city are

pleasantly surprised when they get to the centre, since they usually don't see anything going on.

As we walked through the main shopping area, we passed a Burton's shop and for some reason stopped to look in the window. As Terry glanced at the various clothes on display, I said to him: "You don't have to get nervous, Terry. Just because that dummy over there has got a bullet-proof vest on, don't let that put you off."

I don't think he saw the funny side somehow, because he grabbed my arm and pulled me off up the street back to the car.

We were flying over to Northern Ireland one time and on the plane were Terry Griffiths, Doug Mountjoy and myself. During the flight across, Doug was bemoaning the fact that sometimes people didn't recognise him, and we were pulling his leg about this. He really rose to the bait and kept on emphasising the number of times he had been on television and how surely people must have seen him many times before.

Eventually we landed in Belfast and made our way to the check-in. Now when you land at Belfast you are given a green security card to fill in. Both Terry and I had filled ours in, but waited a few moments for Doug so that we could go through security together.

Doug was still messing about with his card, so we went through ahead of him. I told the chap at the check-in that we were here to play in this snooker tournament. When I found out that he was quite a keen follower of the game, I asked him if he would be prepared to organise a little fun for Doug. He agreed.

Doug duly appeared at the check-in a few seconds later and pushed his way straight through, waving his green card at arm's length as he went past the chap. So the chap called after him, stopped him and made him go back. Doug couldn't understand what the problem was and looked particularly mystified.

"Can I have your name, sir, and have you got any means of identification?"

Now you're supposed to carry this around with you all the time in Northern Ireland. Doug, of course, hadn't and was anyway getting pretty annoyed by this stage. So when the chap again asked him for means of identification, Doug snapped at him: "Yes, bloody me, of course!"

We finally got Doug away from the airport and grabbed a taxi to take us to the Europa – now The Forum – Hotel, where we were booked in. Right in front of the hotel there is a wide road with five or six lanes of

When Doug Mountjoy arrived in Belfast he literally stopped the traffic.

traffic and the three of us had to cross the street. Doug was in the front of the party and stepped out into the road while the rest of us waited at the side to cross. Then a couple of cars started tooting their horns. Doug was delighted. "At last, somebody over here recognises me," he said to us as he turned back, smiling from ear to ear. Then he waved to the cars, which continued to blow their horns.

Unfortunately Doug had failed to realise that he had stepped into the filter lane and the cars that were blasting away were trying to turn left. All they wanted to do was to get him out of the way. I don't think Doug was all that happy when we explained to him what it was really about.

On another trip to Northern Ireland, this time without Doug, Terry and I had agreed to play a particular match for Len Ganley. Now Len – or Len'll Fix It, as he's better known to his friends – wanted to make sure that everything was to our liking and that we were well looked after. So when we arrived he took us to our hotel and said: "Now, would you like a video in the room?" So we said that would be very nice, since we'd be able to relax and watch some films or whatever.

"Fine," he said. "Well, I'll go and fix one up for Terry's room." Then I chipped in: "If Terry's going to have one, then I want one as well." The discussion went on a bit until Len finally agreed to get two. By this time Terry had gone to the reception desk first and had booked in to the best room in the hotel. I was particularly irritated by this, since being in my home country I expected to be given priority treatment. Anyway, Terry had pipped me at the post.

So we made our way to the bedrooms, thinking how pleasant it would be to sit back and watch something on video before the evening match. Finally we got to our rooms, opened the door and went in. Then we noticed that there was no television set anywhere. We couldn't believe it. There was Len making all this fuss about getting us video sets for our bedrooms, when there wasn't even a television in either of them.

This was all too much. So we went back to reception, told them we were checking out and got a taxi to take us to another hotel. The driver then went back to collect our luggage. We made sure the hotel we chose did have a television in each of the bedrooms and left a note for Len to have the videos redirected to the new hotel. It was a polite note, which is more than I can say for Len's reply!

6. Referees I Have Known (and nearly loved)

O ver the years you get to know the top snooker referees pretty well, since they not only adjudicate at the major professional tournaments but also pop up for exhibition matches as well. We have quite a few laughs with them, despite the austere, somewhat daunting manner they adopt around the table.

One particular referee, who shall remain nameless but is one of the biggest in the business and Irish as well, organised for me to play an exhibition match in the town where he lives. When I arrived late that afternoon, I was starving since I hadn't eaten all day. So 'Len' found this little restaurant for me and naturally I invited him to join me in a plate of food.

"Sorry, Dennis, but I mustn't. You see, it's the wife. She's got me on this diet. In fact, there's some fish waiting for me when I get home to keep me going through the evening. But I tell you what. I'll join you for a cup of tea and have a chat while you eat, if that's all right."

So we went in and found a table. When we sat down the waiter came up and left a couple of menus. I picked one up and started looking through it. Having decided what I wanted, I put it down and saw Len browsing through the other one. I said nothing.

When the waiter returned, I ordered up my meal and it was no surprise to find that Len was ordering too. By the time we had finished, he had eaten a starter, main course and a sweet and we both had coffee. When the time came to leave, Len got up and rubbed his stomach. "The wife'll kill me when I get home."

A couple of hours later I met him at the hall we were playing in and I could see he was suffering. Having left me, he then went home and ate his fish as if nothing had happened, because he didn't dare tell his wife that he had already had a three-course meal. I have to admit it was painful watching him at the table, with a waistcoat ready to burst open at any minute.

Although inevitably we take the game very seriously at tournament level, there are times when it is possible to have a little fun. And there is no one better in that situation than referee John Smythe, since once you set John off laughing it's almost impossible to get him to stop. What can make the occasion even more amusing is when he is wearing a radio mike, since then everyone can hear.

I was playing in the Irish championships – I believe it was a quarter-final match, in fact – and was in no trouble at all. Having clinched the match by winning the first frame of the second session, I was able to relax while we played out the remaining frames. Although, as you would expect at that stage, there was not a particularly large crowd in the hall, there was still a reasonable number of people about.

Since by the interval my opponent had obviously decided there was no way he was going to come back from what he regarded as an impossible situation, he had gone to the bar and downed a few glasses of

Guinness. Whether this was to drown his sorrows or a forlorn attempt to revive his game, I couldn't say.

We were back on the table and he had one of the first real chances in the match to pot a few balls. Although the frame was a dead one, he was naturally determined to salvage something from the defeat. He potted a red and then walked round the table for his next shot, which was in fact the blue. However, as he bent down to take the shot he made a particularly rude noise which everyone in the hall heard. There was a deathly silence and the poor fellow went a shade brighter than the red ball. Nobody knew what to do.

Feeling very sorry for him, I looked over sympathetically but by now there was a little smirk on his face. That was enough for me and I burst out laughing, partly to break the embarrassing silence. I then looked at John, the referee, and he in turn collapsed in hysterics. Then, to everyone's relief, the hundred or so people in the hall all joined in and for about five minutes the place was in uproar.

It was one of those amazing moments when the general mood is completely turned on its head by one tiny incident.

A referee was involved many years back in a wonderful little incident with Fred Davis during a tournament in the Leeds area. During one particular match, Fred was in the middle of a break when he noticed something on the cue ball.

Nowadays, as you have no doubt seen on the television, you often get players asking for the ball to be cleaned, in which case the referee gets out the ball marker, sites it, lifts up the ball to give it a good wipe and then replaces it back in exactly the same position on the table.

Unfortunately such aids had not been invented in those days and when Fred asked the referee to wipe the ball, the chap wasn't quite sure what to do about it. He walked over to the table with his white gloves on, and paused to sort out what to do.

After quite a long deliberation, he picked up the ball with his left hand, carefully marking the position of the ball with the first finger of his right hand. That was fine, except that he then had the problem of how to clean the ball with only one hand. There was another moment's pause.

By now the referee was at his wit's end, since he had gone through all the possibilities in his mind and could see no way of wiping the ball and marking the spot at the same time. And Fred certainly wasn't going to suggest anything. Then, in a flash, he lifted his right hand off the table, so that he lost his marker, quickly wiped the ball in both hands and rammed it back down on the table, obviously hoping that no one would notice – except Fred, of course.

When I am playing exhibitions, I try to have a bit of fun with the referees, who are often just local lads or someone from the club. They all carry ball markers nowadays and whenever they are asked to clean a ball they get quite excited, since it draws everyone's attention to them.

I was playing this particular frame, when I thought that I would have some amusement with the referee. So after one shot I turned to him and asked him to clean the cue ball, even though there was nothing on it and the ball hadn't kicked at all. So he got the ball marker out of his pocket, placed it on the table and lifted up the white. "You've been watching television," I said to him. He smiled at me and then turned away to give the ball a quick rub over.

While his back was turned, I picked up the marker as if to check on what type it was. The audience caught it straight away and burst out laughing, at which the referee turned back to see what was going on. Not noticing the marker in my hand, he went to put the ball back on the table and then realised it wasn't there.

For one moment I thought I may have overstepped the mark, but then he smiled back at me and took the marker out of my hand. Fortunately even a referee can see the funny side of it – sometimes!

7. Natural Breaks

O F all the bonuses you get from playing professional snooker, one of the most enjoyable and exciting has been the travel abroad. Although during the snooker season, which lasts roughly from September through to the end of April, most of the time is spent in the UK, there has been plenty of opportunity to go and see the world.

I have had the pleasure of travelling with many of my fellow professionals to as far away as India and Australia, as well as places like South Africa, Canada and America. I should think without exception we have always had some fun together and here I have recalled just a few of those moments.

We used to travel a fair bit to Australia during the early part of the year – normally in January. This, of course, was summer time for them and the weather was really hot. There was a particular hotel we stayed at on one of my first visits to Australia which had a beautiful swimming pool. We used to gather round it, have a chat and go for a swim whenever we wanted to.

I was sitting talking with Graham Miles and Cliff Thorburn when the question of swimming was mentioned. Now neither of us had realised that Cliff Thorburn, despite looking fairly athletic, could not swim. This came as quite a surprise but, not to be beaten, Graham suggested giving Cliff some lessons. Cliff was not particularly keen on this idea, but eventually he did agree to try it out.

*Despite the towel in his hand, Cliff Thorburn doesn't get into
deep water if he can help it.*

For some reason, Graham had failed to bring any swimming trunks with him, so he went into the pool wearing just his Marks & Spencer Y-fronts, which was quite a sight on its own.

Meanwhile I helped a reluctant Cliff into the pool and then sat back at the side to watch all the fun.

Once Cliff was in the water, Graham started explaining to him what he had got to do. He told him to lie flat on the water while he put his hands under Cliff's body to support it. Unfortunately, in his eagerness to teach Cliff to swim, Graham hadn't bothered to check on the position his pupil had adopted in the water and said to Cliff: "Come on now. Kick with your legs."

The trouble was that Cliff's legs were stuck up in the air nowhere near the water, while his head was tipped under it so that he was nearly drowning. After much commotion, Cliff broke free and scrambled back to the side of the pool. As far as I remember, Cliff never went back in the water and I believe Graham gave up swimming tuition at about the same time.

We were playing in a tournament in Sydney and a group of us were staying at the same hotel. We often used to meet up and have breakfast together and on this particular morning there was Rex Williams, Ray Reardon, John Spencer, Doug Mountjoy, Perrie Mans and myself round this large table.

We were chatting away about our personal interests and hobbies outside snooker and Perrie was telling us about his racing pigeons, which he is very keen on and breeds himself. His biggest problem was stopping the cats that roamed about near his home from getting in and killing the birds. It was quite obvious from what he was saying that he disliked the animals intensely. In fact he even went so far as to say that he would kill any cats he saw near his house if he ever had the chance.

Inevitably there had to be a cat lover in the party. Rex Williams had a couple of his own, of which he was very fond, and to say the least was a little upset when he heard Perrie. "Well, that's terrible, Perrie, that's disgusting."

Like many South Africans I have met, Perrie did not have a great sense of humour and he was obviously taking the question of the cats very seriously. "Well, Rex, look at it this way. Just say you bred and

trained racehorses . . .". We all looked at each other. What on earth had racehorses got to do with cats? He went on: ". . . and you were particularly proud of them, not to mention the fact that they were quite valuable. Imagine if a lion broke into the stables one night. What would you do?"

Rex looked at him for a moment, then smiled: "At least I'd find out how fast my horses could run."

At this hotel in Sydney, there was a swimming pool and we would sit out alongside it eating our breakfast and stay there for most of the morning. One day somebody came out looking for Perrie Mans, who hadn't yet joined the party, although by this time it was well after eleven o'clock.

Because there was so little television in South Africa, Perrie used to make the most of it while he was away and had become a real addict. It didn't seem to matter what was on. He would often retire to his room, sometimes as early as five or six in the evening, and we wouldn't see him again till the morning. There was one particular channel that played old films right through the night.

As I said, we were sitting round the pool chatting when this fellow came up and asked: "Has anyone seen Perrie this morning?" Ray Reardon was standing, half-asleep, on his balcony overlooking us and the pool. He heard the chap and called down: "I think he's having a lay-in this morning. He didn't get to bed until eight o'clock last night!"

The poor chap looked totally bemused, although, of course, we all realised what Ray meant.

With all our travelling round the world we have spent a fair bit of time up in the air, and as a result I have got very used to planes and rarely now do I get nerves. There was, however, one flight I was on – coming back from Australia – which did prove rather eventful, but fortunately turned out all right in the end.

We were flying back to England, having played some matches in Sydney, and shortly after take-off I noticed that one of the small reading lights was flashing on and off over on the other side of the plane, a Jumbo 747. I watched it for a while, but there seemed to be nothing untoward happening. Perhaps there was a child playing with the switch. So I turned away and forgot all about it.

About an hour out from Heathrow, suddenly all hell was let loose as smoke started pouring out from the window just by this light. People near the light were jumping up from their seats and the women were

Rex Williams may look solemn here but he's one of the most humorous players away from the table.

beginning to panic. I must admit it was pretty alarming, although by this time we had been flying for more than twenty hours and our little party had sunk quite a few drinks. In fact, we were sitting round playing cards and were in great shape.

Meanwhile the stewards had come running down the plane and were busy ripping out panels round the window to try to locate the cause of the smoke. Obviously there had been a fault in the wiring which had caused it to overheat and eventually catch fire. While the stewards fought to get it under control, Rex Williams looked over his large glass of gin and tonic at them.

Now Rex may appear one of the more serious of the players when he's on the table, but in fact he's quite a funny man away from it. Suddenly he burst out laughing, which seemed extraordinary since everyone else was getting very alarmed by the scene on the other side. "Oh look," he said, "we seem to have got a steward's enquiry here."

To give Rex his credit, he certainly managed to take some of the tension out of the situation and I'm glad to say the problem was soon under control and we arrived at Heathrow in one piece – and much relieved, I may add.

I was able to enjoy a much more relaxed flight to Australia in the company of Graham Miles and Cliff Thorburn. I used to spend quite a bit of time with the two of them while on tour and therefore got to know them both very well.

Graham's main problem when flying was that he could never sleep properly and therefore used to land after a long flight, such as to Australia, feeling absolutely exhausted. Strangely enough, on this trip he went out like a light for some reason or other, leaning up in the corner seat against the window.

Cliff and I, who were sitting next to him, decided that we would have a bit of fun and test just how sound asleep he really was. So we started piling anything we could find on to him, without waking him up. First we laid newspaper over the top of him and then took off his shoes and socks and put these on his head. There were books, magazines, paper cups and plates – in fact, whatever we could lay our hands on.

Eventually we got the pile almost to the ceiling and left it there for at least half-an-hour, during which time he never moved a muscle. When anyone walked past, they stopped and had a good laugh at Graham, who looked a right sight. He, of course, hadn't a clue about what was going on and we managed to remove everything before he woke up.

When he finally stirred, Cliff and I were laughing away, but never let on why and Graham couldn't understand either why some of the passengers continued to give him strange looks. At least we had proved one thing – that Graham was quite capable of going sound asleep on a plane at last.

Whether Graham Miles ever took any advice from Doug Mountjoy or not, I don't know. But Doug never had any problem about sleeping. On the contrary, when he goes to sleep you just can't wake him up. Twice I played a similar trick on him as we had done to Graham. On both occasions we happened to be on tour in Australia.

We were in a hotel lounge, having had some coffee, when Doug just nodded off. He was sitting upright in his chair with his arms folded at the time. So I got his cup and saucer and balanced them on his head, then sat back and timed it. Believe it or not, the cup and saucer were still there thirty-five minutes later, which only goes to show just how sound a sleeper Doug can be.

A group of us had gone into this fish restaurant in Sydney called Doyles to have a meal. It's a great place if you like fish, since they serve every type imaginable. So we sat down and enjoyed an excellent meal. Doug Mountjoy was in the party and, sure enough, after getting through his meal he leant back and fell fast asleep in his chair.

The rest of us moved quickly into action, stacking all sorts of bits and pieces on his head and in his arms. There were fish bones of all shapes and sizes, prawn heads and tails – you name it, we piled it on.

Naturally this caused a great deal of amusement round the restaurant, since nobody there had ever seen anything quite like it before. To begin with the waiters didn't appear particularly happy, since I suspect they anticipated trouble. But we were soon able to put their minds at rest and eventually they too joined in the fun.

When it came to leave, Doug was still fast asleep. So we removed all the evidence and spent the next few minutes trying to wake him up. We finally got him up off his chair and out of the restaurant.

Then we had to get a taxi back to the hotel, since there was no way he was going to walk there in his state of drowsiness. So I propped him up against a nearby tree as I went to look for a cab. Eventually I found one and came back to get Doug, who – yes, you guessed it – had only fallen back to sleep leaning against this tree.

As you will no doubt have gathered, we get up to plenty of things beside snooker when we travel about the world and often receive invitations to join in other activities. When we were playing in Sydney we were offered a day out with a local angling club just outside the city to try our luck.

I was with Graham Miles and Cliff Thorburn at the time and since none of us had ever been fishing before, we decided this would be an ideal opportunity to try our hand at it. So we happily accepted.

The club had arranged to pick us up from the hotel and the car took us over there, where we were ushered into this large rescue boat that they use. I suppose there must have been a dozen or so in the party altogether.

The lads on the boat explained to us what we had to do to catch the local fish – I believe they were called silvertails. All I ever knew about fishing before then was that you used a rod and line. In this case there was no rod and we were given this spool-like object which we had to hold. On the end of the line there were lumps of prawn and other pieces of fish.

It all seemed pretty complicated to us, but we said we'd have a try and threw our lines over the side of the boat. The idea was to drop the line down into the water so that the bait was fifteen to twenty feet under and then jiggle it about until you got a bite. When you felt a tug, they told us, pull your line in. That was all very well in principle, I thought, but what about in practice?

In fact there were loads of fish about and as I looked around everyone seemed to be catching some. Mind you, it was Botany Bay and I had heard all the usual stories about fishing there.

Graham was up the front of the boat and as I looked over I noticed he had caught four fish. I wasn't doing too badly either, having managed to land three. When you pulled the fish in, fortunately there was someone on hand to bash it on the head with a mallet and take it off the hook. I have to admit, I wouldn't have liked doing that part at all.

I then turned to Cliff, who was fishing next to me. I could see he was getting a bit fed up, since he had been jiggling his line about for well over half-an-hour and hadn't had a single bite. So I thought I'd have a look over the side to see what was going on. Then I burst out laughing.

"What's the matter?" Cliff snapped at me.

"Just you have a look," I chuckled.

So Cliff leant over and there was his line, all tangled up, with the bait hanging about a foot out of the water.

It was hardly surprising he hadn't had a bite all morning. I suppose he might have been lucky enough to catch a flying fish, although I refrained from mentioning that. Cliff was so disillusioned by all this that he pulled in his line and spent the rest of the trip watching the others pull the fish in.

Graham Miles has provided us all with lots of laughs over the years, particularly since he has this uncanny knack of getting things wrong and causing no end of confusion, without even meaning to. Nowhere is this more easily done than abroad, particularly with the different languages and habits.

We were in India at the time, playing in Bombay, and had decided to go out and do some shopping, particularly to find some souvenirs and presents to take back home. Graham's a great one for shopping, so I let him lead the way. Just below the hotel we were staying at there was a large market and this was where we headed for.

The trouble in India is that you cannot just wander along and browse quietly at each shop you come to. As soon as you stop to look, somebody rushes out and tries to pull you inside. We paused outside this particular place and immediately a little fellow in a turban came out, chattering away and trying to get us to go inside.

Fortunately Graham stood his ground: "No thanks, I'm just having a look." But the little Indian was not to be put off by this and kept on at us. Graham pretended not to notice and was looking at the stuff in the front – small pieces of ivory, different statuettes and things like that. Eventually he thought: "I'd better buy something, just to get this chap off our backs."

So he turned to the Indian, who I think at this stage was about to give up anyway, and pointed at one of the small ivory figures. Using his best pidgin English, he said: "How much that piece there?" The Indian looked, then burst out laughing. Graham turned to me: "What's the matter? What's he laughing at?" I just shrugged my shoulders.

Then the Indian started to explain that he couldn't sell him the piece he wanted because it was part of a chess set and he didn't want to break it up.

After all the previous bartering, poor Graham couldn't believe it. He grabbed my arm and moved on down the market, a sadder and wiser man.

I shall never forget another incident in India with Graham. We had been playing an exhibition match and had been invited on to a dinner party at this private club afterwards. We had a marvellous evening and were well looked after by our hosts. Inevitably things went on fairly late and it was well after midnight when the party broke up.

We had to get back to our hotel, which was some miles away, and the fellow who had organised the evening said that his son would be pleased to run us back. So we gathered our bits and pieces and followed him out to the car park. There were six of us in all, since he was dropping off some other people as well.

If you have ever been to India you will know that the cars there are virtually all the same – probably two or three different makes and that's about it. So how anyone manages to find the right one, I shall never know. Anyway we finally got to the car and all piled in.

As the driver drew away, there was this bumping noise as the car lurched over on one side. He looked out of his window, then turned back to us. "I'm terribly sorry," he said in that inimitable Indian accent, "but we have got a flat wheel."

Graham, who was sitting on the same side at the back, looked out of his window and said: "No, you're OK, it's only flat at the bottom!"

I did feel sorry for the driver. It took him quite a while to work out exactly what Graham had said.

Since snooker has become very much part of my life – and happily so – it is somewhat disconcerting to find that there are occasions when others will refuse to accept that I am a snooker player. Although there may have been times in my career when I may have wished to be anything but one, I certainly don't need others to tell me so!

Thanks to players like Cliff Thorburn, Kirk Stevens and Bill Werbeniuk, Canada has been put well and truly on the international snooker map. However there was a period, not too long ago, when the game was scarcely recognised in that country, as I found out to my acute embarrassment.

In the early days, I used to play quite a bit over there, particularly in Toronto, and I shall never forget my first visit. Customs control for those who flew in was pretty tight and the officials were very thorough in their interrogation of visitors to the country. Whether it was because I was carrying this strange-looking case I appeared particularly suspicious, I do not know, but I was slightly concerned when I was ushered into this small cubicle and had to face a barrage of questions from a customs lady, who had obviously never heard the word 'snooker' in her life.

When I asked her what the problem was, she told me: "Well, Mr Taylor, we understand that you are here on business, but we are having trouble deciding what category to list you under."

I then explained that I was a professional snooker player and had come to play in a tournament. Unfortunately this only seemed to confuse the issue further.

She left me sitting in this cubicle for about twenty minutes while she went off to make more enquiries. Eventually she came back in, and with obvious relief and some satisfaction at having solved the problem, said: "I think we can get round this, Mr Taylor. We've had some wrestlers come to Canada to work, so we've decided to let you in under that category."

I have to admit that the connection between wrestling and snooker did escape me. But in my eagerness to get out of the clutches of the customs, I happily agreed.

Still, who knows? If I ever find I can't make a living as a snooker

player any more, I could always try getting a job as a wrestler in Canada. At least they'd let me in without too much bother.

After my first visit to Canada I found it a lot easier to be let in, and on one of my trips I played in a tournament at the Canadian Exhibition Centre, a vast complex used for all sorts of events. For one reason or another we were unable to play in the hall normally used for sporting events such as the snooker tournament I was involved in. Instead, they had put up this large tent outside. It was at the end of July or early August, as I recall, and the weather was particularly hot. Inside the tent, however, it was absolutely boiling.

Fortunately the organisers had had the foresight to erect four huge fans, one in each corner, which were directed down towards the snooker table. Although this brought very welcome relief in one respect, it caused quite a bit of chaos for me in another direction.

When you are playing snooker, you always like to look neat the tidy. So you make an extra effort to smarten yourself up. In my case this includes washing my hair and giving it a blow-dry and then putting lacquer on it to prevent it flopping about or, worse still, falling over my eyes.

Despite my normal preparations, the fans were so powerful that after a while my hair literally stood up on end, completely destroying my concentration.

In all my career as a professional snooker player, without doubt these were the four worst fans I have ever had!

I shall always remember one trip I made to Canada, since in the party was the legendary Joe Davis. It was, in fact, one of the last trips he made abroad. Apart from making it memorable from that point of view, I had a little bit of fun with Willie Thorne before I flew back to England.

We were sharing a room in the hotel we all stayed at and had been there about ten days. While the rest of us were flying back home, Willie had decided to stay on a little longer. So we said our farewells and left for the airport.

When the party arrived, much to our annoyance there was some problem with the flights. Although nobody quite knew what was wrong, from what we could gather there was some trouble with either the customs or air traffic control. Whatever it was, we couldn't get the flight we were booked on and the airline had to put us into the nearby hotel for the night.

The next morning we were waiting in the hotel lounge for news of our flight home. I was chatting away to John Spencer and saying how fortunate Willie had been to arrange to stay over, since at least he had missed all the aggravation. Then I decided to give him a ring.

When I phoned Willie at his hotel, he obviously assumed that I was now back in England. So I didn't give the game away and went on for about quarter-of-an-hour chatting away about different things. He obviously thought it was a bit strange, not to say extravagant, ringing from England and spending all this time on the phone. Eventually I said to him: "Now, Willie, I nearly forgot. The main reason for ringing you is that I've just unpacked and I can't find one of my black socks. The only thing I can think of is that I left it in our hotel bedroom. Possibly it fell under the bed or somewhere. Do you think you could have a look for me?"

"Hang on a minute," said Willie. "I'll put the phone down and go and have a quick look for it."

In fact he spent near enough five minutes rummaging around looking for a black sock, before he came back on the phone. "Dennis, I'm terribly sorry, but I can't find your sock anywhere. Are you sure it isn't in your case with the rest of your stuff?"

Poor Willie was getting quite concerned about the whole affair, particularly at what it was costing me for a phone call. I decided I had to come clean.

"Look, Willie, don't worry about it, honestly. In fact I'm ringing you from the hotel near the airport. We never got off the ground last night." There was silence on the other end of the phone. "You don't really think I'd ring you up all the way from England over a measly black sock, do you?"

Willie was none too pleased at hearing the whole thing had been a wind-up from the start.

On one of our other tours to Canada, we had another Irish player in the party. Now this particular chap was a great television addict and therefore in his element, since in Canada you could pick up a whole host of programmes from many different stations. Not only did you get Canadian ones but a lot from America as well. With such a choice, you could watch television twenty-four hours a day if you wished.

Our friend was really impressed by this and one day, shortly before we were due to leave for home, he pulled me to one side: "This is fantastic, Dennis. There's nothing like it at all where I live. Tell you what I'm going to do. I'm going to buy one of these television sets and take it back home with me. That way, I can watch all these extra stations – and right through the night if necessary."

Of all the invitations I have been offered, I must say I am grateful I wasn't around when Rex Williams and John Pulman, who were playing out in South Africa, were invited to try their hand at water-skiing.

A group of people from a water-skiing club, who had been watching them play snooker, came up afterwards and insisted that they should have a go. Despite showing considerable reluctance, the two were finally persuaded to give it a try and the next morning they were collected from their hotel and taken down to the waterside.

When they arrived, quite a crowd were there to watch them perform, much to both players' embarrassment. But everything had been laid on, so there was no getting out of it. After a short period of instruction on the principles of the sport, it was time to have a go. Rex was the first one on the skis, with John driving the speedboat.

Now John hadn't driven too many speedboats before, let alone towing somebody on skis behind one. When you turn on the water the speed of the skis is virtually double that of the boat. So if the boat is travelling at, say, 30 mph, then the person on the skis is doing nearer 60 mph. Neither John nor Rex realised this, and as John swung the boat round, there was poor Rex hurtling towards the shore at some incredible speed, convinced he had had his lot. Miraculously he managed to keep his feet – or rather his skis – and survived.

Then it was John's turn on the skis and it was quite a sight seeing him in the water, struggling with this pair of skis with his glasses on – since John always wears them. He eventually got himself ready, with the skis pointing up in the air. The idea here is that as the boat sets off, you have to pull yourself up on to the skis until they are flat on the water and you are upright.

That is all very well in principle. Unfortunately, as the boat set off, the skis remained upright but there was no sign of John. As Rex looked round, all he could see was a pair of skis sticking up in the air, with this figure thrashing away in the water behind, trying desperately to pull himself upright.

I gather John was mightily relieved to get back on to dry land and spent the rest of the trip wholeheartedly concentrating on his snooker.

I have to admit that my feelings about visits to South Africa have been fairly mixed as well, particularly when I recall one trip that proved to be one of the most exhausting I have ever been on.

A group of us happened to be out there at the time they were holding the South African Grand Prix, and everywhere was packed out. Although there were plenty of hotels in the area, we had trouble finding accommodation and eventually I ended up sharing a room with Eddie Charlton.

It may surprise you to learn that Eddie is a fitness fanatic and every morning I had to put up with the same routine. Eight-thirty on the dot and there was Eddie, bouncing out of bed and throwing open the windows, where he'd stand doing his deep breathing as I buried my head under the pillow just wishing he'd do his exercises somewhere else.

Then he would pick up the phone and ring down to reception and, in typical Australian fashion, order up breakfast. I wouldn't have minded that too much if I had been allowed to choose what I wanted. Not a bit of it. He never asked me what I wanted but insisted that I ate what he had. He was determined to get me on to his fitness course as well.

A few minutes later there would be this knock on the door and in came our breakfast, if you could call it that. There was fresh fruit salad, strawberry-flavoured yoghurt and a large glass of milk each. Can you imagine it? Once was more than enough for me, but I had to get this lot down for ten days on the trot.

After we had finished, it was into the bathroom for a quick shower, then on with the shorts and out into the fresh air, where we'd set off jogging. I must admit I used to do some running and quite enjoyed it. But this was nearly two years ago and I was well out of practice. Eddie was quite an expert, of course. In fact, he runs up to ten miles a day with no trouble at all.

So off we would set, from outside the hotel. You can imagine the strange looks we used to get as we walked through the foyer. Although I must admit I did improve over the period, for the first few days the going was pretty tough. I managed to keep up the pace for the first mile or so, but gradually I fell behind as he kept going. Mind you, when I finally arrived back at the hotel I was only something like six minutes adrift,

which I thought was pretty good going, considering my condition at the time.

Unfortunately Eddie was not convinced and used to tell everyone quite a different story. He was sure that once he was out of sight I stopped jogging, waited a while and then caught a taxi back to near the hotel, completing the last few yards on foot as though I had jogged all the way.

Try as I may, I could never persuade him otherwise. Mind you, it was a good idea. I wish I had thought of it at the time.

In spite of all the snooker you see on television these days, we professionals don't play the game fifty-two weeks of the year – normally just fifty! Since most of us have families that we see precious little of, we do make the effort occasionally to get away from it all – or almost.

A little while ago, Doug Mountjoy, Terry Griffiths and myself teamed up with our respective families and embarked on a trip to the States. Needless to say, one of our ports of call was Orlando, Florida, to have a look in at Disneyworld. Anticipating problems in deciding who did what and when, we agreed to take it in turns to be in charge of the holiday party. One day I would play leader, the next Terry and so on.

We spent several days at Orlando and went to Disneyworld more than once, since there was so much to see. This time it was Doug's turn to take charge, which with thirteen in the party was quite an ordeal, I can tell you. We had been walking for about three-quarters of an hour when Doug came across the miniature train that runs through the massive complex. "Aha," he thought. "This is just the job. We can see a lot more from this."

So we all piled on to the train and off we went. Finally it came to a stop and, as we looked around, it all seemed rather familiar. Then we twigged what had happened. We had only jumped on the train returning to where we had originally come in. Having taken forty-five minutes to walk through the complex, we had done the return journey in less than five.

Doug was certainly not the most popular person in the party as we all trooped back along exactly the same route we had walked less than an hour before.

While we were in the States, it wasn't unknown for us to slip into the odd bar. Normally there was no problem, since most people in America haven't even heard of snooker, let alone recognise any of us players.

We made one mistake, however, by walking into an Irish bar where we were instantly recognised by the exiled barman and were immediately surrounded by well-wishers and autograph hunters. We joined in the spirit of things in more ways than one and eventually got roped into an impromptu talent competition that was being organised.

Since neither Terry nor I were prepared to admit that we had any ability in this direction, we put Doug forward. In fact, although he gets little chance to exercise his hidden talents when playing snooker, Doug is quite a good singer – when he's sober. His favourite songs are 'Danny Boy' and 'She Wears My Ring'. The problem is that when he's had a few, he tends to get them mixed up and ends up singing the two together.

When it came to his turn, he decided to start with 'Danny Boy', which he was giving an excellent rendering of, perhaps enough to put him in with a great chance of winning, when his voice completely cracked halfway through. Sadly he was relegated to third place – so you can imagine how good the fourth place was! But it wasn't a bad effort, really.

8. Wearing the Golfer's Hat

I suppose if you were to ask the average professional sportsman what other game he played in addition to his own, a good percentage would say golf. In this respect snooker players are no exception, since I and many of my colleagues do frequent the other green when we can.

Personally I enjoy it since it gets me out into the open air and I find the whole atmosphere very relaxing. Of course there are times, as with any other sport, when things can become very frustrating. Equally you can pull out one of those shots in a million and spend the rest of the week – in some cases, the year – talking about it and boring everyone to tears.

As far as I'm concerned, if there's one thing better than a good fishing story then it's a golfing one.

I was invited to a Pro-Celebrity golf day at Accrington some years back. It was particularly convenient since I live only about four miles from there and had played the course quite a lot. I remember it being a beautiful sunny day, just right for a game of golf.

Unfortunately I arrived a bit late and had little time to spare on some practice swings. I more or less had to go straight on to the first tee. We were playing foursomes and I made my way to the start, where the other three were waiting. If I remember right, the first hole was a par three 178 yards. In the past I had used either a five or a three wood, depending on which way the wind was blowing.

I think I was asking directions to the clubhouse bar!

I went up to take my shot and, possibly through not having had any real practice, I topped it badly. As I stood there watching it, I saw it bounce three times and smack this fellow straight in the mouth. It really scared me, since I didn't know what damage I had done to him. I was certainly very relieved when I saw him collect his trolley and move on. It was only then that I realised he was a member of my team, which only added to the embarrassment.

As the fellow walked round, his lip was getting bigger and bigger and I felt so awful that I could hardly hit the ball for the next few holes. He must have been in agony, the poor chap.

Anyway, as it turned out he was OK by the end of the round. But he nursed a pretty sore mouth for at least a week afterwards. It couldn't have happened playing snooker . . . could it?

I didn't have too much luck that day. My brother, Martin, who doesn't play much golf but had agreed to turn up with me, was caddying. I won't repeat his comments after that first shot off the tee. Anyway, I had driven off at the second and was fortunate to get quite close to the green. So I asked him for the sand wedge so that I could play a chip shot, hopefully up and near the flag. He started rummaging through my bag, but couldn't find the wedge anywhere.

"It must be in there somewhere," I said.

"If it is, I can't find it," he replied.

"Well, you must have dropped it somewhere back there." So I sent him back down the second fairway to look for it.

By this time the next team was coming up towards us. So Martin went up and asked them if they had seen a club lying on the course. One of them happened to be Willie Morgan, the former Manchester United player.

"Have you by chance seen a sand wedge lying about?" But neither he nor any of the others had. While my brother carried on down the fairway, I decided to have another check in the bag and, sure enough, there it was.

It could only happen to the Irish, I thought to myself! This first-class caddy had removed the cover when he pulled out the three wood for my tee shot and, because he didn't want to keep it in his hand, had stuck it on top of one of the other clubs, which happened to be the sand wedge. So when we went through the clubs, we had both assumed that what was under this cover was another wood.

I have had the pleasure of playing at La Moye Golf Club in Jersey, where Ray Reardon is an honorary member. We went over to put on a snooker exhibition at the club and I was invited to stay with a chap called Barry Will, a top hairdresser from London who has lived on the island for many years.

Barry is a great Jewish character and always quick to have a bit of fun when the occasion arises. Since we were not due to appear until the evening, he suggested we went out and had a round of golf in the afternoon. I was only too pleased to accept.

We were going quite nicely and I was thoroughly enjoying the course when Barry suddenly let out this cry. As I turned round I could see him pulling back his shoulders and he was obviously in some pain. "What's the matter?" I asked.

"Someone's just hit a ball right between my shoulders," he said. Then he swung round and called out: "Whoever hit that ball, I'll sue him for £6,000."

Almost at once this voice shouted from the distance: "Four!"

Barry turned to me: "You heard him. I'll take it!"

Wherever I travel I always take my golf clubs with me, just in case. Normally there's a chance you can get to a course, even in India, for example.

On one of our trips out there we were staying in Bombay. Having inquired as to whether we could play golf, we were directed to this course just outside the city. John Spencer was with me and we got a car to take us to the course.

As you can imagine, it can get pretty hot out there and anyone who goes out to play is automatically given a caddie, which is a great relief. They also have other boys positioned round the grassy areas to stop the balls for you. This may sound like cheating, but there is a very practical reason for doing it. At certain times of the year, the place is infested with snakes and it is very much in your own interests not to go trampling through the rough to retrieve your ball! I must admit that when we heard

about this both John and I had second thoughts about going out at all.

Anyway we set off round, concentrating a lot more on direction than length, for obvious reasons! John is quite a useful golfer and usually plays off 12 or 13. Unfortunately, however, the inevitable happened and he put one of his shots into the rough, wide of one of the lads. Naturally enough, he wasn't too keen on having to go into the grass and play his next shot. But the lad showed him where the ball had gone and he

carefully felt his way through the grass, prodding and poking away with one of his clubs – just in case.

His ball was lying under this large tree and, having stepped carefully up to it, John positioned himself for the shot. Just as he was about to play, still obviously very nervous about the possibility of a snake appearing, something large and damp dropped right on top of his head from out of the tree and started running down his neck. He let out the most deafening yell I have ever heard in my life and I was surprised he didn't die of a heart-attack. I must admit I almost did.

Then this huge bird flapped its wings and flew out from one of the branches directly above him.

John forgot all about the mess and the smell. He was only too pleased that what had landed on him was not a snake.

You'd be surprised what a dangerous life we snooker players really lead.

During the Jameson Whiskey International at Newcastle a couple of years back, I was involved in one of the most amusing rounds of golf I have ever played. The challenge came from Des Heather, the public relations manager for Jameson, who hails from Dublin and can be quite a character. He fixed up the match with David Harrison, the promoter of the tournament, as his partner. I played with Cliff Thorburn.

Although David boasted a handicap of 28, he could hit a ball pretty hard when he connected properly, and Des played off 11. So, despite the fact that Cliff enjoyed a handicap of 7 and I was then playing off around 20, it promised to be a pretty tough match.

We had left Des to sort out the handicaps, but unfortunately none of us could agree on his final calculations. So, to settle it, Des said: "I tell you what, lads. We'll take six shots – and two throws." Then Cliff looked at me and I knew exactly what he was thinking. What's all this about throws? We've never heard of this one before.

Des realised immediately our problem: "Well, it's quite simple. The club I normally play at in Ireland has this handicap system where you can introduce a number of throws."

I pulled Cliff to one side: "I'm sure he's up to something, although I can't work out what it is. Anyway, Des can't throw the ball that far so we might as well agree to it." Eventually a reluctant Cliff was persuaded, and we went out.

Everything was going fine until the fifth hole, when I chipped a shot from about 120 yards from the green and finished up about four feet from the pin. I was walking up to the green with Cliff, feeling particularly pleased with myself and confident that we had won the hole, when I noticed Des, who had gone on to the green ahead of us, stoop over my ball. I gave Cliff a nudge. We quickened our pace and as we arrived on the green Des picked up my ball and said: "Now we're taking our first throw." And with that he chucked my ball a long, long way out of bounds.

Cliff and I looked at each other in total amazement, then laughed. We'd certainly fallen for that one good and proper.

It always amazes me, looking back, how we ever managed to finish that round, but eventually we did reach the eighteenth green, much to my surprise – and I'm sure Cliff's as well. But the fun wasn't over yet, by a long way.

As I said, we were by now on the final green, the largest on the course, and Cliff was preparing to take his putt. With a 7 handicap, the Canadian is no mean golfer, partly due to the accuracy of his putting which he studies almost as carefully as he does his shots on the snooker table. While he was lining up the shot, Des walked over to tend the flag. Neither of us were paying much attention, although every so often Cliff glanced

up to where the flag was. Finally he was ready and hit the ball, a shot of about twenty yards.

It was a great effort, since Cliff managed to roll his ball to within six inches of the flag. Then Des looked up at him and said: "Hard luck, Cliff." He then walked about six paces to the left of where the ball was and put the flag back in the hole.

Oh well, you can't win them all. But it was a great afternoon's golf, nevertheless. And the one consolation was we did have a few miniatures tucked away inside our golf bags with which to drown our sorrows.

Last year we were out playing tournaments in New Zealand and in between matches we managed quite a bit of golf. Most of the time I played with Cliff Thorburn and Tony Knowles, another keen golfer.

One morning we decided to have a round together and, after breakfast, we grabbed a cab from our hotel to the nearby course. I was sitting in the front, with Cliff and Tony in the back.

During the drive out of town we were chatting away about snooker and the subject of slow play just happened to crop up. Cliff was forced to admit to Tony that he did take quite a while over individual shots, though it wasn't deliberate.

Then the conversation turned to golf, which, as I have already mentioned, Cliff is pretty good at. In fact, if he were able to practise more, his golf could probably be as good as his snooker.

Cliff happened to drop into the discussion the time factor over shots in golf. "I don't know why it is, but in snooker I just have to take time over each shot. With golf, on the other hand, I actually play the ball quite quickly. I simply can't understand why that should be."

Tony, who had been listening to this with a smile on his face, replied: "It's quite easy really, Cliff. In golf you know what you're doing!"

Goodness! If that's true, I hope Cliff never finds out on the snooker table.

9. Over the Mike . . .

I know for a fact that some players don't particularly enjoy commentating and I have to admit it can prove a little daunting at times. The real problems come when you're doing a live broadcast. Once something's been said, there's no taking it back or editing it out. You therefore have to think carefully about what you are going to say before you say it, although that is easier said than done, as many a commentator knows to his regret.

All in all, you can have quite a lot of fun when you've got the mike in front of you. However, given the choice I would far rather be down there on the table playing than sitting in the commentary box watching.

I do a fair amount of commentating, probably a lot more than I would really like, but it can be great fun working alongside such people as John Pulman, six times world champion and a person who is very knowledgeable about the game.

While we were in the commentary box at one particular tournament, he told me about an episode many years before at a British Legion club up in Cumbria. The odd thing about this was that I had only recently been there myself and was the first professional to have done so since John's visit.

You may probably have gathered from this fact that John had not gone down too well with the committee there, which was a great pity since he has got a terrific sense of humour and I can only assume that the people there had simply taken the incident in quite the wrong way.

John Pulman – snooker player, commentator and chimney sweep.

John had turned up for an exhibition match dressed immaculately, as a professional player would normally expect to do on such an occasion, with his dress-suit and all the trimmings – and, naturally, carrying a long case inside which was his cue. As he walked in through the front door, he was approached by the president and secretary of the club and one of them asked: "Oh, are you Mr Pulman by any chance?"

John immediately replied: "Well, who did you think I was – the bloody chimney sweep?"

I am sure they would recognise him the next time he walked through that door.

We get plenty of letters during the season from all kinds of people asking about different – and often very personal – things. One in particular that always makes me chuckle was in fact sent to the BBC's David Vine, from this dear old lady who told him that she was an avid snooker fan and watched it all the time. He showed me the letter she had written, which read:

Dear Mr Vine,
Now I understand why the game of snooker takes so long. When a player pots the balls into the pockets and is walking round the table with his back turned, that fellow with the white gloves quickly takes them out and puts them back on the table again.

John Pulman was again in the commentary box during one particular match in the Yamaha Organs International when Steve Davis was working his way through what turned out to be a huge break. I was sitting alongside John and was quickly doing some arithmetic.

"I have worked out that there's a possible break of 127 on here, should Steve take all the colours. This, of course, would equal the previous highest break, currently made by Cliff Thorburn. Incidentally, the highest break for the tournament carries a prize of £500 plus a Yamaha organ."

At which point in the commentary, John broke in to interrupt my comments and added, very dryly: "I wonder what you could do with just half an organ?"

I was playing through a frame in this tournament and I remember Rex Williams was in the commentary box with Ted Lowe. I hit a shot and, without a doubt, it was one of the worst positional shots I have played in my life. It was a real nightmare. The white stopped right behind these other balls so that the only way I could play it was by cueing right over the top.

There was no point in crying over this desperate situation, so I said out loud so that all the crowd could hear me: "That's exactly where I wanted to be." At which the crowd, who had been very concerned for me and my shot, burst out laughing.

Ted Lowe picked up the atmosphere straight away and added: "Of course, Dennis Taylor is not only a great snooker player but he's also a great comedian." At which point Rex chipped in: "He'd have to be a comedian to play a shot like that!"

The oldest hand in the game must be Whispering Ted Lowe, who in many ways epitomises the game and has done great service for the sport over the years he has had the mike. I hope he will forgive me for reminding him of the time he was commentating on a match in which Fred Davis was playing.

Rather like myself, Fred doesn't particularly like using the rest and will sometimes, when he can, change hands. In this particular match, he was faced with a very awkward shot which he first tried to play right-handed, as he would normally do. He pulled his leg up over the corner of the table, but even so he found he wasn't able to reach it comfortably. So he pulled himself back off the table and swopped the cue over into his left hand.

Ted was watching this from the commentary box and obviously got carried away with it all. "You know, Fred Davis is sixty-seven years of age now and he's obviously a little too old to get his leg over."

No sooner had he let the words slip when he realised what he had just said. Desperate now to talk his way out of a very embarrassing situation, he added: "As you can see, he prefers to use his left hand instead."

Talking of commentators, we all come in for a bit of stick from the public every so often and probably some of it is justified.

There is a woman who lives in my area who keeps ringing up the local radio station complaining about the snooker commentators. Virtually every time there's a televised tournament, she's on the phone ripping them to pieces.

During one particular call she made, she told this programme presenter live over the air: "They make me sick. They just keep on talking. If only I had a black and white television, I'd turn the sound down!"

I know what she means and if she'd like to give me her address I'll see what I can arrange!

When I do a spell of commentating with John Pulman, I have said we usually manage a laugh or two between us. On one occasion my namesake David was playing and was faced with a very nasty shot. The balls had got jammed up round the top pocket, with the black very close to the cluster. Whichever way he went, there really wasn't a shot on anywhere.

We were discussing this over the mikes when John suggested: "The only shot he can really play here with any safety is the ricochet." To which I added: "Yes, that's the one perfected by that famous Irish snooker player many years ago – Rick O'Shea!"

On that theme, I recall there were several other notable players whose names come to mind immediately. There was that Chinese champion Kew Ing Wel and, talking of people from the Far East, I once played against an Indian who hit the ball particularly hard, in a style reminiscent of Alex Higgins. His name was Rama Din.

Nearer home we shouldn't forget that rather fortunate Scottish champion Jock McKew, while the most erratic man I've played against was the Welshman Dai O'Rea. It was a job to keep him at the table.

Ray Reardon looking nervous as midnight approaches again.

It is just as well that Ray Reardon has a sense of humour, since I have to admit I've let a few comments slip over the mike when he's been playing. If only he didn't have this uncanny resemblance to a certain gentleman from Trannsylvania.

Ray was well behind in one match I was commentating on, and the

camera happened to pan in on his face as he sat waiting to get back on the table. I felt I had to say something to justify the camera's move.

"Well, there's no doubt you can never write this man off. He's been a great champion. In fact, he's been known to come back from the dead many times before."

It was getting towards the end of that match and Ray was well out of the frame, needing snookers. His opponent, on the other hand, was potting everything he went for. Another red went down and the camera turned to pick up Ray's reaction. I commented at the time: "Well, that looks like being the final nail in the coffin of Ray Reardon."

I happened to be in the commentary box for another match that involved Ray, and in this particular frame there had been a lot of safety play. After one long bout of it, Ray picked up a loose red and potted it.

By this stage we were getting desperate for anything to say and without thinking I piped in: "Well, that's first blood to Ray Reardon."

One of the most amusing incidents in the commentary box came when I was doing some work for Irish television during the Benson & Hedges Irish Masters. Alongside me was Ray McNally, a fine actor who has appeared in a lot of television plays as well as films. He happened to be working at the Abbey Theatre in Dublin at the time, and popped in occasionally to add his comments. Ray's a great character – and no mean snooker player either.

I remember watching this chap attempting a shot across the table at the green, which was on its spot. It wasn't a particularly difficult pot, but he missed it all the same. I commented afterwards: "The reason he missed that shot was because he was playing across the nap of the cloth and didn't make the necessary allowance."

I then paused and was about to explain to the viewers about the nap of the cloth in case they did not understand what I meant, when Ray took the microphone off me. And before I could explain, he said over the air: "For those of you who don't know about the nap of the cloth, it's like the fur on a pussy cat's back!"

He never got any further with the explanation. I almost fell out of the commentary box laughing and he was obviously in no state to carry on. I could just imagine all the old ladies listening in their armchairs at home, calling their cats and sitting them on their lap, then stroking them to find out what the nap of the cloth was like.

Fortunately, the producer sent in our reliefs at that point.

10....Taking the Mick

I should imagine more jokes are told about the Irish than just about any other nationality in the world. When you stop to think about it, we've got to be pretty good-humoured to take them all.

But, quite seriously, it doesn't bother me at all. And just to prove it, here are a few jokes about my countrymen. I will say one thing, though. Irish jokes are a lot funnier when they're told by the Irish.

Paddy was out looking for a job when he passed this building site. So he went up to the foreman and asked him if there were any jobs going.

"Well, there could be. Can you make tea, Paddy?"

"Of course I can," Paddy replied. "I worked for Wimpeys for four and a half years, didn't I?"

Then the foreman asked him: "And can you drive a fork-lift truck?"

Paddy looked surprised. "Jesus," he said, "how big's the kettle, then?"

In fact Paddy did get the job on the building site and started the next day. Soon after he arrived, the foreman called out to him: "Paddy, can you nip up to the top of the yard and bring me down a wheelbarrow?"

So off Paddy went and came back five minutes later with two wheelbarrows, one inside the other.

The foreman looked at him. "What's the matter with you, then? Are you stupid or something? I only asked for one wheelbarrow."

Paddy replied: "I know you did, but you didn't think I was going to carry it down, did you?"

Some days later, while Paddy was still on this building site, he had this terrible accident where both his ears were ripped off. He was rushed to hospital where he had to stay for three weeks. While he was in, the foreman paid him a visit to see how he was getting on. When he came back, he had a long chat with Mick, one of Paddy's mates.

"Now Mick," he said, "Paddy's going to be coming back to work on Monday, so whatever you do, don't mention his bloody ears. He's very sensitive about them, so make sure you don't talk about them at all."

So when Monday came round and Paddy arrived back at work, Mick went up to him. "How are you then, Paddy?"

"Oh, not so bad, you know."

Then Mick said to him: "I see your eyesight's improved, then."

Paddy gave him a strange look: "What are you talking about, Mick?"

"Well, you're not wearing your glasses, I see!"

Paddy didn't last long on the building site after that and decided to look for another job, something totally away from the building line. So he applied for this job with a big posh company and a few days later went for an interview. He was shown into this large posh office and sat down. The fellow then got out his pen.

"Can I have your name, please?"

"Certainly. It's Paddy Macnamara."

"Fine. Could you spell that for me?"

Paddy paused, thought for a minute then got up from his chair. "Oh hell, you can stuff your job. I didn't want it anyway."

By now Paddy was right down on his luck, so he thought the only thing to do was to try and pick up a few quid by doing odd jobs. So he went to this posh housing estate and started knocking on doors. Eventually he came to one house and this fellow answered the door.

"Excuse me for troubling you, sir, but would you be having any odd jobs you want done?"

The fellow took pity on him and said: "Yes, I think I can find you a job. Can you paint by any chance?"

"Oh yes sir," Paddy replied. "I can paint all right."

"Fine. Well, if you go round the back, you'll see this porch. I want it painted green. You'll find the paint and some brushes round there."

"Thank you, sir. You're very kind. I'll paint the porch for you, all right." And off Paddy went round to the back of the house.

A couple of hours later, Paddy reappeared round the front, where this fellow is sitting in a deckchair reading the paper. Paddy went up to him.

"All finished, then?"

"Yes sir. All done. And, though I say it myself, you'll never see a better job, no sir."

So the fellow gave him £10.

"Thank you very much sir."

As Paddy was walking back down the drive, he turned round and

called back to this fellow. "By the way, sir, that Porsche round the back isn't a Porsche. It's a Mercedes!"

Paddy decided one day he wanted a dog, so he went off to the pet shop and got this puppy. The trouble was that it kept on wetting the carpet.

So he decided he'd have to teach it to pee in the gutter. Unfortunately, as he was training the dog, he fell off the roof and killed himself.

Two of my fellow countrymen came over a few years ago to visit me in Blackburn and while they were here decided they'd like a game of snooker. So they went down to the club to see the manager, who was a very good friend of mine. He got them a free table and a set of balls and left them to play.

After more than five hours on the table, he thought he'd better go over and see how they were getting on. When he got over to the table he realised they hadn't managed to pot a single red. The trouble was they'd left the triangle over the reds.

Paddy had just been home to see his family in Ireland and he'd got off the train in Euston and was walking up the road carrying these two great suitcases. A chap walking towards him stopped him: "Excuse me, but have you got the right time?"

Paddy was a bit annoyed at having been stopped, but he put down his suitcases and looked at the watch on his wrist. "Well," he said, "according to this it's six forty-five and fifty-one seconds."

The chap looked more closely at the watch and said: "Heh, that's quite a watch you've got there."

"Yes," said Paddy, "it is. There's a little switch here which gives me a choice of Radio 1 or Radio 2. Then there's this one here which, if I turn it round and then pull it out, controls this aerial here. With that I can get BBC1 and BBC2 if I want. Then if I turn the switch here, there's another, bigger aerial which gives me all the ITV stations and Channel 4."

The fellow looked at him in amazement. "That's incredible. I bet it cost you a fortune."

"Not really," said Paddy. "I picked it up off a friend for £6."

"Heavens. I don't believe it. There's got to be a snag somewhere," the fellow went on.

"Yes, there is. See these two suitcases? They're the bloody batteries for it!"

Paddy had just won a fortune on the Pools and he was talking to his friend, Mick. "You know, Mick, the first thing I'm going to do is buy myself a really good watch. I've always wanted one of those."

Mick replied: "Well, Paddy, you know the best watches in the world are made in Switzerland."

"That's right, Mick, so they are." And the next day Paddy flew out to Switzerland.

When he arrived there, he walked past all these shops with windows full of clocks and watches and eventually he decided to go into one. There inside were rows of glass cases, all crammed full of watches. As he walked along past them, he noticed one he particularly liked. So he called a chap over and said: "I'll be having that one, please."

The chap looked at him rather surprised and said: "Well, sir, are you sure it's that one you want?"

"Of course it is. I said it was, didn't I?"

"Yes, sir, you did. But did you know it was made of solid gold with a 23-carat diamond movement and is guaranteed not to lose a second in twelve months?"

"So?"

"Well, sir, that watch will cost you £50,000."

"That's fine. I'll take it. If it is what you say it is and it does what you say it does, then I'll buy it."

So Paddy took his watch and flew back home. That evening he was sitting in the front room watching television with his little lad. He had made up his mind not to look at his watch until 'News at Ten' came on for him to check it, so he kept the cuff of his shirt sleeve over the watch and waited. When the news appeared, he pulled back the cuff and looked at the watch, which read half-past nine. Then he turned to the lad and gave him the most almighty smack round the ear.

The lad looked startled and bemused. "What's up, Dad?"

"What's up? You've been messing about with that bloody television set again."

_____

Paddy failed to turn up for work one day and the foreman went up to his mate, Mick. "Where's Paddy, then?"

"Oh, he's broken his leg."

"How did he break it?"

So Mick said: "He was raking leaves in the garden."

"How can you break your leg raking leaves?"

Mick replied: "Apparently he fell out of the tree."

Paddy was weaving his way home one night along the canal bank, steamed out of his mind. He'd been in the pub all evening and drunk sixteen pints of Guinness and as many whiskies. As he staggered along, he noticed this fellow shouting for help in the water and about to drown. Anyway, all that drink had given him extra courage so he decided to jump in and rescue the fellow.

Feeling pretty pleased with himself, he swaggered on home and went to bed. About three in the morning there was this banging on the front door, so Paddy went down to see what was going on. When he opened the door there were two policemen standing there. One of them said: "Ah, Mr Murphy, isn't it, Paddy Murphy?"

"That's right, I am that."

"Well, Mr Murphy, we have reason to believe you rescued a drowning man from the canal tonight. Is this true?"

"That's perfectly correct, officer, as a matter of fact. But you don't have to worry yourself about that. I don't want any medals or anything for it."

The policeman replied: "Well, God love you, Mr Murphy, but we aren't here to give you any medals, anyway, I'm afraid. We just came to tell you that you needn't have risked your life as you did to pull that man out of the water."

"Oh, and why's that?"

"Because, Mr Murphy, the gentleman then went and hanged himself from a lamp-post."

"That's not quite true, officer. In fact, I put him there myself to dry."

Paddy was coming to England for the first time and was on his way to the airport when he bumped into some neighbours of his. It was Mr and Mrs Dunn from across the road.

"Where are you off to, Paddy?" Mrs Dunn asked.

"Why, to England, of course."

"Ah, that's wonderful, Paddy. When you get there, can you do us a favour?"

"Of course, Mrs Dunn. What is it?"

"Well, when you get to England, if you see our son, Neillie, would you tell him to write to us? We haven't heard from him in over two years now."

"Certainly I will, Mrs Dunn. But do you know where he lives?"

"Well, I think it's London, WC1."

Paddy caught his plane and landed at Heathrow. As he was walking through the airport, he passed this door which had WC on it. So he thought he'd better have a look in and when he got inside he saw this row of doors. So he went to the first one and there was somebody inside. So he called out: "Excuse me, but are you Neillie Dunn?"

To which the fellow inside said: "Yes, I am, but I can't find any paper."

"Well," said Paddy, "that's a pretty poor excuse for not writing home to your mother."

Paddy and Mick were sitting in a snooker club and opposite them was a great big mirror. While they were there talking, Paddy happened to look up and then said to Mick: "Be Jesus, Mick, that's amazing."

"What's that," said Mick.

"Well, there's two fellows sat over there that look just like you and me."

"That's incredible, that," said Mick.

Then Mick gets up and starts walking towards them. "Where are you going, Mick?"

"Well, I thought I'd go over and buy them a drink."

Paddy grabbed him by the arm and pulled him back. "Quick, sit down, Mick. One of them's coming over to buy us one."

Paddy and Mick finally gave up waiting for their drink and went to play a game of snooker. When they got to the table, they saw this meter.

"What's this for?" said Paddy.

"Well," said Mick, "you have to put some money in, I think, and then the lights come on."

"Right," said Paddy. "Now, let's see. What does it take? Oh, we need 10p pieces."

"That's a pity," said Mick, "cos I've only got 50p pieces on me."

Paddy thought for a minute and then came up with an idea. "Tell you what, Mick. If we file off the corners, we can use those as a 10p piece."

When I won the World Championship I decided to look for a new manager. So I got out the yellow pages and was thumbing through the lists of names when I came across this firm of Murphy, Murphy, Murphy and Murphy. "That sounds just about right for me," I thought, and so I gave them a ring.

This man answered and I said: "Can I speak to Mr Murphy, please?"

"Sorry, he's not here anymore. He's retired."

"Oh, that's a pity. Then can I speak to Mr Murphy?"

"No, you can't. I'm afraid it's his day off today."

I thought for a minute. "Oh, well in that case can I speak to Mr Murphy, then?"

"Sorry, he's on the other line."

I was getting pretty frustrated by this stage. "Well, can I speak to Mr Murphy then?" The man replied: "Mr Murphy speaking."

Enough, I think, of Irish jokes. Perhaps it's time for somebody else to be on the receiving end. When I'm telling jokes during an exhibition match, I usually get a bit of stick from the audience and invariably it's a Scotsman leading the way. Which reminds me of the Scotsman who owned a snooker club. One day he was taken seriously ill and died. In his will he left his son two snookers.

Not long ago I was involved in the Russell Harty Show over in Belfast and there were three Irish comedians due to appear, with me doing a few trick shots. In fact the programme marked sixty years of the BBC in

Northern Ireland and, just for a change, the producer asked if anyone knew any gags against the English that they could tell. Amazingly enough, none of them could come up with one on the spur of the moment. That, in itself, tells its own tale! So I volunteered the following:

"What's black and blue and floats in the Irish Sea?"

"An Englishman that's just told an Irish joke."

Paddy and Mick had taken a special holiday excursion to New York to see the sights. They had been walking miles and were coming along Fifth Avenue when Paddy disappeared down a flight of steps in the middle of the pavement. This just happened to be the entrance to an underground station.

A minute or so later Paddy finally appeared up the other side, where Mick is standing waiting for him. "Where the hell have you been then, Paddy?" asked Mick.

"Be Jesus," replied Paddy. "I've just seen the most fantastic basement, Mick. You just wouldn't believe it. These Americans certainly know how to live, that's for sure. Boy, you just want to see his train set!"

This fellow was snooker mad – literally living, sleeping and eating the game. One day he came out in this terrible rash and couldn't work out what the trouble was. So he went to see his doctor.

"From what I can see," the doctor told him, "it must be something to do with your diet. Have you been eating anything strange recently."

The chap looked very embarrassed and then said: "Well, doctor, I have to confess that I have this terrible craving for snooker balls."

"And you eat these every mealtime instead of food?"

"Yes, doctor."

"OK, let's take yesterday, for example. What did you have for breakfast?"

"Let me think. Yes, I just had a couple of reds, a yellow and a brown."

"And for lunch?"

"Well, for lunch I wasn't that hungry and I got by on two reds again, a yellow, a brown and a blue."

"Incredible. And what did you eat for dinner?"

"Actually I went mad and had five reds, a yellow, a brown, a blue and a pink. Oh yes, and I finished up with a black."

The doctor scratched his head and thought for a moment. Then he said: "Well, I think I know what your trouble could be. You're not eating any greens."